FUTURE
English for Results

2

WORKBOOK with AUDIO CD

Janet Raskin

Series Consultants

Beatriz B. Diaz
Ronna Magy
Federico Salas-Isnardi

PEARSON
Longman

Future 2
English for Results
Workbook with Audio CD

Pearson Education, 10 Bank Street, White Plains, NY 10606

Staff credits: The people who made up the *Future 2 Workbook* team, representing editorial, production, design, and manufacturing, are Peter Benson, Elizabeth Carlson, Aerin Csigay, Dave Dickey, Nancy Flaggman, Irene Frankel, Michael Kemper, Michael Mone, Rebecca Ortman, Liza Pleva, and Barbara Sabella.

Cover design: Rhea Banker
Cover photo: Kathy Lamm/Getty Images
Text design: Barbara Sabella
Text composition: Rainbow Graphics
Text font: 13 pt Minion

Illustration credits: Steve Attoe: pp. 37, 73; Kenneth Batelman: 60, 112; Laurie Conley: 27, 65, 107, 132 (bottom middle and right); Stephen Hutchings: pp. 27, 129, 131; André Labrie: 29, 75, 81, 135; Robert Sadi: 21, 39; Neil Stewart: 136; Anna Veltfort: 3, 53, 85, 137.

Photo Credits: Page 5 Brand X/SuperStock; 6 Shutterstock; 8 Shutterstock; 10 Shutterstock; 13 Tetra Images/Alamy; 14 Shutterstock; 17 Blend Images/Alamy; 18 Reed Kaestner/Corbis; 23 Shutterstock; 26(1) Paula Ludwig/age fotostock, (2) Shutterstock, (3) Shutterstock, (4) Shutterstock, (5) Adam Hunter/Tiger Advertising/www.tigeradvertising.ca, (6) Dynamic Graphics/Jupiterimages, (7) Frederic Cirou/Jupiterimages, (8) Photos.com/Jupiterimages, (9) Adam Hunter/Tiger Advertising/www.tigeradvertising.ca; 28 BigStockPhoto.com; 31 Adam Hunter/Tiger Advertising/www.tigeradvertising.ca, Paula Ludwig/age fotostock, Dynamic Graphics/Jupiterimages, Frederic Cirou/Jupiterimages; 34 Shutterstock; 35 Shutterstock; 38(1) Shutterstock, (2) Elenathewise/Dreamstime.com, (3) TongRo Image Stock/Alamy, (4) Shutterstock, (5) Purestock/Getty Images, (6) Jack Hollingsworth/age fotostock, (7) Shutterstock, (8) Blend Images/Alamy; 45 Shutterstock; 46 Diana Lundin/iStockphoto.com; 49 Shutterstock; 52 BigStockPhoto.com; 58 Shutterstock; 62(1) Image Source/SuperStock, (2) Comstock/Jupiterimages, (3) Royalty-Free Division/Masterfile, (4) Peter Byron/PhotoEdit, (5) Daniel Templeton/Alamy, (6) Shutterstock, (7) Stephen Simpson/Getty Images, (8) Hurewitz Creative/Corbis, (9) Image Source/Getty Images; 70 Charles Platiau/Reuters/Corbis; 74(A) Royalty-Free Division/Masterfile, (B) Shutterstock, (C) Shutterstock, (D) Shutterstock, (E) Pixtal/SuperStock, (F) image100/Jupiterimages, (G) image100/Corbis, (H) Custom Medical Stock Photo/Alamy, (I) Shutterstock; 82 Shutterstock; 84 Kathleen Finlay/Masterfile; 86(1) Anderson Ross/Blend Images/Corbis, (2) Andersen Ross/Brand X/Corbis, (3) GOGO Images/SuperStock, (4) Creatas/age fotostock, (5) Robin Nelson/PhotoEdit, (6) Index Stock Imagery; 87(TL) Monkey Business Images/Shutterstock, (TR) Shutterstock, (BL) Andersen Ross/Brand X/Corbis, (BR) Michael Jung/Shutterstock; 89(L) Hongqi Zhang/123RF, (M) Somos Images/Corbis/Glow Images, (R) Corbis; 92 China Photos/Getty Images; 93 Hulton Archive/Getty Images, Childers Michael/Corbis Sygma, Bettmann/Corbis, Kenneth James/Corbis; 94 StockLite/Shutterstock; 97 Shutterstock; 98(1) Tom Stewart/Corbis, (2) wavebreakmediamicro/123rf.com, (3) Royalty-Free Division/Masterfile, (4) PhotoAlto/Alamy, (5) Fotolia.com, (6) Karelnoppe/Fotolia, (7) Hallgerd/Fotolia., (8) Blend Images/Alamy, (9) Rhoda Sidney/The Image Works; 99 Shutterstock; 106 Shutterstock; 109 DesignPics Inc./Photolibrary; 114 Shutterstock; 115 Shutterstock; 117(fresh) Shutterstock, (frozen) mediablitzimages Limited/Alamy, (can) Photos.com/Jupiterimages, (pears) Shutterstock, (juice) mediablitzimages Limited/Alamy, (oranges) Shutterstock, (salmon) Shutterstock, (steak) Shutterstock; 118 Shutterstock; 120 Radius Images/Alamy; 124 Blend Images/Alamy; 126 Photos.com/Jupiterimages; 128 Shutterstock; 130 North Light Images/age fotostock; 133 Shutterstock; 134(1) Digital Vision Ltd./SuperStock, (2) Randy Faris/Corbis, (3) Jupiterimages/Stockbyte/Getty Images, (4) David Bacon/The Image Works, (5) Taylor Jorjorian/Alamy, (6) Michael Krasowitz/Getty Images; 135(L) Royalty-Free Division/Masterfile, (M) Frederic Cirou/Photolibrary, (R) Photos.com/Jupiterimages; 139(T) Blend Images/Alamy, (M) David R. Frazier Photolibrary, Inc./Alamy, (B) Hola Images/Alamy; 142 Steve Skjold/PhotoEdit.

ISBN-13: 978-0-13-199151-4
ISBN-10: 0-13-199151-5

Contents

To the Teacher

The *Future 2 Workbook with Audio CD* has 12-page units to complement what students have learned in the Student Book. Each Workbook unit follows the lesson order of the Student Book and provides supplemental practice in vocabulary, life skills, listening, grammar, reading, and writing. Students can complete the exercises outside the classroom as homework or during class time to extend instruction.

The Workbook Audio CD is a unique feature of the Workbook. It provides practice with conversations, grammar, and life skills competencies. In addition, the audio CD includes the readings from the Workbook so students can become more fluent readers.

UNIT STRUCTURE

Vocabulary

Practice focuses on the vocabulary presented on the first spread of the unit. Typical activities are word and sentence completion, labeling, and categorizing. Some lessons include sentence writing to reinforce the lesson's vocabulary, and some lessons include personalized exercises.

Grammar and Listening

Grammar is the main focus, with listening practiced as well. Grammar is practiced in contextualized exercises that include sentence completion, sentence writing, sentence scrambles, matching, and multiple choice. Listening activities include listening comprehension, listening dictation, and listening to check answers. Some lessons include vocabulary exercises to reinforce the new vocabulary taught in the lesson. Some lessons include personalized activities.

Life Skills

Practice focuses on functional language, practical skills, and authentic printed materials such as schedules, labels, and receipts. Realia-based exercises are featured on these pages, which also include vocabulary, grammar, listening, and personalized activities.

Reading

Each reading page includes a new reading related to the unit topic. The reading is also on the audio CD so students can listen as they read. Each article is followed by a reading comprehension exercise and a personalized writing exercise.

ADDITIONAL RESOURCES

At the back of the Workbook, you will find:
- Audio Script
- Answer Key
- CD Track List
- Bound-in Audio CD

ORIENTATION

The Workbook, like the Student Book, includes an orientation for students. Before the students use the Workbook for the first time, direct them to the To the Student material on the next page. Go through the questions and tips with the students and answer any questions they may have so they can get the most out of using the Workbook.

To the Student

LEARN ABOUT YOUR BOOK

A PAIRS. Look in the back of your book. Find each section. Write the page number.

Audio Script ＿＿＿   Answer Key ＿＿＿   CD Track List ＿＿＿

B PAIRS. Look at page 154. Find *Answers will vary*. What does *Answers will vary* mean?

C CLASS. Where is the Audio CD?

D CLASS. Look at page 5. What does mean? What does *Play Track 2* mean?

TIPS FOR USING THE AUDIO CD

CLASS. Read the tips for using the audio CD.

- For all exercises, listen to each track many times.
- For dictation exercises, use the pause button ⏸ so you can have more time to write.
- After you finish the unit, for more listening practice, play the audio again and read the audio script in the back of the book at the same time.
- Also, for more listening practice, listen to the conversations and readings when you are in the car or on the bus.

WRITING TIPS

CLASS. Read the writing tips.

- Start sentences with a capital letter.
- End statements with a period (.).
- End questions with a question mark (?).

For example:

＿＿＿＿ My name is Jack. ＿＿＿＿

＿＿＿＿ What's your name? ＿＿＿＿

Unit 1: Making Connections

Lesson 1: Vocabulary

A WORD PLAY. Complete the chart. Use the words in the box.

> curly   a goatee   heavy   long   a mustache
>
> short   shoulder-length   tall   thin   wavy

Facial hair	Hair type	Hair length	Height	Weight
a beard	straight	short	average height	average weight

B Complete the sentences with words from the boxes. Put the words in the correct order. Then look at the people. Write the name of each person.

> black   short   straight

1. Suyin has __short__, __straight__ __black__ hair.

Ⓐ

> curly   black   short

2. Ahmed has _____, _____ _____ hair.

Ⓑ

> brown   wavy   long

3. Claudia has _____, _____ _____ hair.

Ⓒ

Suyin

> shoulder-length   blonde   straight

4. Saul has _____, _____ _____ hair.

Ⓓ

C Look at the picture. Write words to describe the people.

    Michael   Cha-Ram   Alexandra

    short hair   _____   _____

_____   _____   _____

_____   _____   _____

_____   _____   _____

D MAKE IT PERSONAL. Think of four of your friends, family members, or classmates. Write words to describe them.

Diego: short, average weight, curly black hair

1. _____

2. _____

3. _____

4. _____

A Complete the conversations. Underline the correct words.

1. **A:** Marta and Clara look alike!

   B: Yes, they both **has / <u>have</u>** blue eyes and red hair.

2. **A:** What does your brother look like?

   B: He **is / has** average height and a little heavy.

3. **A:** Are those girls your cousins?

   B: Yes, that's Gloria and Miladys.

   A: Wow! They **are / have** very attractive.

4. **A:** Is the man with the goatee your husband?

   B: No, he **isn't / aren't**. My husband **don't have / doesn't have** a goatee!

5. **A:** Look! That's Nina.

   B: The blond? No, Nina **doesn't have / don't have** blond hair.

   A: Well, she **is / has** blond hair today!

   B: Oh, yeah! That *is* Nina!

B Complete the sentences. Write the correct forms of *be* or *have*. Use contractions for the negative sentences.

1. Mark (**not**) _____doesn't have_____ straight hair.

2. Nicole and Pilar _____ long, curly hair.

3. Mi-Hee _____ average height.

4. Mr. Johnson _____ a beard.

5. Carlos and Fernando (**not**) _____ heavy.

6. Mr. and Mrs. Johnson _____ good-looking.

7. I (**not**) _____ blond hair.

C 🔘 **Play track 2. Listen to the conversation. Circle *True* or *False*.**

1. Carol has blond hair.   True   False

2. Carol has long, straight hair.   True   False

3. Carol has blue eyes.   True   False

4. Carol is average height.   True   False

5. Carol is heavy.   True   False

6. Carol is pretty.   True   False

D **Look at the picture. Write sentences to describe the people.**

Guillermo   Usain   Ziwei   Andrey   Lars

1. *Andrey has short hair.* _____

2. _____

3. _____

4. _____

5. _____

A Look at the driver's license. What do the abbreviations mean? Write the words.

Florida *The Sunshine State*

DRIVER LICENSE

S514-172-80-844-0

GONZALEZ, NINA S
150 CLEARWATER ROAD APT. 5
TALLAHASSEE, FLORIDA 32317

DOB: 08-16-78   SEX: F   HT: 5-6

Nina S Gonzalez   WT: 135   HAIR: BLK   EYES: BRN

ISSUED: 02-13-09   EXPIRES: 02-13-13

1. APT _____apartment_____

2. DOB _____

3. F _____

4. HT _____

5. WT _____

6. BLK _____

7. BRN _____

B Look at the driver's license in Exercise A again. Complete the statements.

1. Nina's last name is _Gonzalez_____.

2. Nina lives on _____ Road.

3. Nina lives in the state of _____.

4. Nina was born in the year _____.

5. Nina is _____ feet, _____ inches tall.

6. Nina has _____ hair.

7. Nina has _____ eyes.

C Complete the application. Use the information on Nina's driver's license in Exercise A.

DRIVER LICENSE / ID CARD APPLICATION

DMV

(Please print in blue or black ink only)

LAST NAME	FIRST NAME	MIDDLE INITIAL	SUFFIX (JR., SR.)

DATE OF BIRTH (mm-dd-yyyy)	HEIGHT	WEIGHT	SEX (CIRCLE)	HAIR COLOR	EYE COLOR
	FT. IN.	POUNDS	MALE FEMALE		

RESIDENCE ADDRESS	STREET	APT. #

CITY, STATE, ZIP CODE	SIGNATURE OF APPLICANT
	X *Nina S Gonzalez*

D Complete the application for yourself. Use your own information.

DRIVER LICENSE / ID CARD APPLICATION

DMV

(Please print in blue or black ink only)

LAST NAME	FIRST NAME	MIDDLE INITIAL	SUFFIX (JR., SR.)

DATE OF BIRTH (mm-dd-yyyy)	HEIGHT	WEIGHT	SEX (CIRCLE)	HAIR COLOR	EYE COLOR
	FT. IN.	POUNDS	MALE FEMALE		

RESIDENCE ADDRESS	STREET	APT. #

CITY, STATE, ZIP CODE	SIGNATURE OF APPLICANT
	X

E MAKE IT PERSONAL. What applications have you completed?
Check (✓) the boxes.

❑ apartment rental ❑ driver's license ❑ ID card ❑ library card

❑ school enrollment ❑ supermarket card ❑ other: _____

Ⓐ Complete the sentences. Underline _and_ or _but_.

1. Tina tells great jokes <u>**and**</u> / **but** she's very funny.

2. Mr. Lee isn't friendly **and** / **but** he's bossy.

3. Guillermo is cheerful **and** / **but** his brother is moody.

4. Andre tells great stories **and** / **but** he's very interesting.

5. Sandra has black hair **and** / **but** her children have brown hair.

6. My boss is laid-back **and** / **but** he's friendly.

7. David and his father are heavy **and** / **but** his mother is slim.

8. Melissa doesn't have blue eyes **and** / **but** her sisters have blue eyes.

Ⓑ Read what the people say about their personalities. Write two sentences about each person. Use _and_ and _but_.

"I'm friendly. I'm a little shy. I think I'm funny. My friends say I tell great jokes."

1. **Oscar**

"I'm outgoing. I'm a little bossy. I'm talkative. I really like to tell stories."

2. **Chung-Ho**

Oscar is friendly but he's a little shy.

Oscar is funny and he tells great jokes.

_____

_____

"I'm shy. I get nervous when I meet people. I love to travel. I love to visit new places."

3. **Jason**

"I am hard-working. I like to relax after work. I'm laid-back. My husband says I'm moody!"

4. **Noelle**

_____   _____

_____   _____

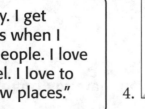

C Read the two sentences. Write one sentence. Use *too* or *either*.

1. Jun is thin. Hwang is thin. <u>Jun is thin and Hwang is, too.</u>

2. Mr. Lee isn't tall. Mr. Peters isn't tall. _____

3. Sally's hair isn't curly. Olivia's hair isn't curly. _____

4. Alexander is handsome. His brothers are handsome. _____

5. The boys aren't shy. The girls aren't shy. _____

6. My sister is outgoing. I am outgoing. _____

7. Kevin isn't quiet. You aren't quiet. _____

D Look at the information in the chart. Write sentences about the people. Write three sentences with *too* and three sentences with *either*.

Name	Weight	Height	Personality
Lydia	thin	tall	funny
Viktor	average weight	tall	laid-back
Kwon-Su	heavy	tall	bossy
Luz	average weight	short	funny
Edwin	thin	average height	laid-back

1. <u>Lydia and Viktor are tall and Kwon-Su is, too.</u>

2. _____

3. _____

4. _____

5. _____

6. _____

BEFORE YOU READ

Look at the titles and photos in the article. Predict: What is the article about?

_____

READ

💿 **Play track 3. Listen. Read the article.**

Protect Your
Identity

Last year, Susana Montoya got a call from a bill collector. The bill collector said she owed $1,200 for an unpaid credit card bill. She was surprised. She didn't have a credit card. Susana was a victim of identity theft. A thief used her name and social security number to open a credit card account.

What is identity theft?

Identity theft is when someone uses another person's name and personal information. It is important to protect information such as your name and social security number. Thieves can use this information to get a credit card in your name. They can also borrow money from a bank, rent an apartment, or open a telephone account in your name. When it is time to pay the bill, the thieves won't pay. Then the bill collectors will come looking for you.

How does identity theft happen?

Thieves can get personal information in many ways. They look through garbage for papers such as bank statements or credit card bills. They steal purses and wallets. They ask for personal information by phone or e-mail, pretending to be from a company you do business with.

How can you stop identity theft?

In the U.S., thieves steal the identities of 9 million people every year. But there are ways you can protect yourself. Here are some tips.

- Don't give out personal information by phone, mail, or e-mail unless you know who you are dealing with.
- If you move, call your bank and credit card company and change your address.
- Don't use your social security number as identification. Don't keep your social security card in your purse or wallet.
- Shred personal documents like credit card receipts, bank statements, medical papers, and bills before you throw them away.

Source: http://www.ftc.gov

CHECK YOUR UNDERSTANDING

A Read the article again. What is the main idea of the article? Circle the letter.

    a. Never give personal information over the phone.

    b. It is important to protect your personal information.

    c. Thieves can use your personal information to open a bank account.

B Answer the questions with information from the article.

    1. What are four things that thieves can do with your personal information?

       _____   _____

       _____   _____

    2. What are three ways that thieves can get your personal information?

       _____   _____   _____

C Complete the tips with information from the article.

    1. Be careful when people ask you to give personal information by _____,

       mail, or _____.

    2. Tell your bank and credit card company when you change your _____.

    3. Don't keep your _____ in your purse or wallet.

    4. Shred documents like _____, bank statements, _____,

       and bills before you throw them away.

D MAKE IT PERSONAL. What do you do to protect your identity?

_____

_____

_____

A Write questions. Put the words in the correct order.

1. (Pam / friendly / is) <u>Is Pam friendly?</u>

2. (from Mexico / are / Mr. and Mrs. Garcia) _____

3. (you / are / married) _____

4. (your school / where / is) _____

5. (how old / the students / are) _____

6. (is / who / your teacher) _____

7. (is / your birthday / when) _____

8. (your name / what / is) _____

B Complete the conversations. Use *am, is, are, am not, isn't,* or *aren't.*

1. **A:** Are we late for class?

   B: No, we ___<u>aren't</u>___. We're on time.

2. **A:** Is the English class in room 12?

   B: Yes, it _____. It's on the first floor.

3. **A:** Are you in this class?

   B: No, I _____. I'm in the morning class.

4. **A:** Are your children outgoing?

   B: No, they _____. They're shy.

5. **A:** Is Son from China?

   B: No, he _____. He's from Vietnam.

6. **A:** Are you the teacher?

   B: Yes, I _____. My name is Mr. Gordon.

7. **A:** Are Mr. and Mrs. Park talkative?

   B: Yes, they _____. They're very outgoing.

C Read the answers. Complete the questions.

1. **A:** Where _is Ernesto from?_

   B: Ernesto is from Chicago.

2. **A:** What _____

   B: My phone number is 845-555-4398.

3. **A:** When _____

   B: English class is at 2:00.

4. **A:** How old _____

   B: My daughter is eight years old.

5. **A:** What _____

   B: My country is very beautiful.

6. **A:** Where _____

   B: I'm from El Salvador.

D Imagine you are meeting a new classmate. What questions could you ask?
Write three *Yes / No* questions and three information questions. Use *be*.

> _Where are you from?_

1. _____

2. _____

3. _____

4. _____

5. _____

6. _____

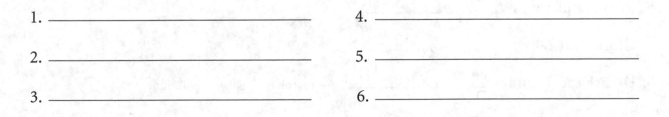

E MAKE IT PERSONAL. Look at the questions you wrote in Exercise D.
Answer the questions about yourself. Use your own information.

1. _____   4. _____

2. _____   5. _____

3. _____   6. _____

Lesson 1: Vocabulary

A WORD PLAY. Which family members are related to you by birth? Which are related to you by marriage? Complete the chart.

aunt	brother-in-law	daughter-in-law	fiancé
granddaughter	husband	mother	mother-in-law
nephew	niece	sister	wife

Related by birth	Related by marriage
aunt	brother-in-law

B Look at the Miller family tree. Write the family relationships.

1. Daniel and Sandra _husband and wife_

2. Charles and Gloria _____

3. Monica and Gloria _____

4. George and Sandra _____

5. Monica and Sally _____

6. Joseph and Tommy _____

7. Gloria and Sally _____

8. Daniel and Tommy _____

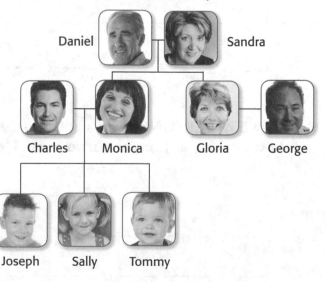

The Miller Family

Daniel   Sandra

Charles   Monica   Gloria   George

Joseph   Sally   Tommy

C **Look at the family tree in Exercise B. Complete the statements.**

1. Daniel and Sandra are Gloria's _parents_.

2. Joseph and Sally are Monica's _____.

3. Monica is George's _____.

4. Charles is Tommy's _____.

5. Daniel is Joseph's _____.

6. Joseph is Sally's _____.

7. Sally is Tommy's _____.

8. Joseph is Gloria's _____.

D **MAKE IT PERSONAL. Draw your own family tree. Start with one pair of your grandparents. Write each person's name and his or her relationship to you.**

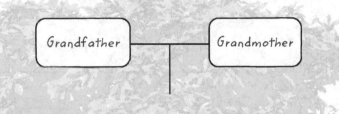

Grandfather — Grandmother

A **Complete the sentences. Write the correct forms of the words in parentheses.**

1. Sheila (**live**) ___lives___ in California. She (**work**) _____ in a hospital. She (**have**)

   _____ a son.

2. Mr. and Mrs. Wang (**live**) _____ in New York City. They (**work**) _____ in a

   flower store. They (**have**) _____ two children.

3. Chin-Hwa (**live**) _____ in Los Angeles. He (**work**) _____ at a bank. He (**have**)

   _____ a wife and a new baby.

4. My sister and I (**live**) _____ in a small town. We (**have**) _____ jobs after school.

   We (**work**) _____ in a restaurant.

B **Write negative sentences. Use *don't* or *doesn't*.**

1. Alicia and Carlos live on Franklin Street.

   _Alicia and Carlos don't live on Franklin Street._____

2. Camille works in a hospital.

   _____

3. I have two jobs.

   _____

4. Deshi and Bao live in Florida.

   _____

5. You have four sisters.

   _____

6. Manuel lives downtown.

   _____

C Complete the paragraph. Write the correct forms of the words.

My sister and I _____live_____ in Boston. I
                         1. live

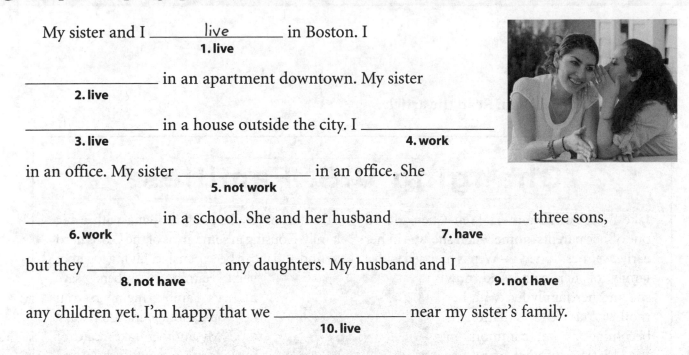

_____ in an apartment downtown. My sister
    2. live

_____ in a house outside the city. I _____
    3. live   **4. work**

in an office. My sister _____ in an office. She
                            5. not work

_____ in a school. She and her husband _____ three sons,
    6. work   **7. have**

but they _____ any daughters. My husband and I _____
    8. not have   **9. not have**

any children yet. I'm happy that we _____ near my sister's family.
                             10. live

D 🄾 Play track 4. Listen to the conversation. Then read the sentences. Circle *True* or *False*.

1. Roberta has a new job.	**True**	**False**
2. Roberta works in a department store.	**True**	**False**
3. Roberta doesn't live near her job.	**True**	**False**
4. Roberta works in the evening.	**True**	**False**
5. Roberta has children.	**True**	**False**
6. Roberta's husband works in a hospital.	**True**	**False**

E MAKE IT PERSONAL. Think of two members of your family. Write
sentences about each person's life and work.

> My brother Sam lives in Los Angeles. He has two kids.
>
> He works in a school.

1. _____

2. _____

READ

🔘 **Play track 5. Listen. Read the article.**

Changing U.S. Families

Like most Americans, Ya-Wen Chen moved out of her parents' home when she was in her early twenties. Today, Ya-Wen is married with a family of her own. And now she and her family live with her mother. Ya-Wen's situation is becoming more common in the U.S. The number of homes that include children, parents, grandparents, and sometimes great-grandparents is increasing. By the year 2015, experts believe that the number of three- and four-generation households will continue to grow.

Families of new immigrants are the most likely to live together. In many cultures, a traditional family has four generations living under one roof. "My parents moved to the U.S. from China," explains Ya-Wen. "Back home, it wasn't unusual for a big family to live together."

There are many benefits to living with a big family. Housing in some areas of the U.S. is hard to find and it can be expensive. Living together helps family members save money. Family members can help one another in other ways, too. "My mother takes care of my kids so I can go to school and get a degree," says Ya-Wen. "My mother and my children have a close relationship. That's very good for all of them. And when my mother needs to go to the doctor, I can take her. We take care of one another."

However, living with a big family can be difficult. As Ya-Wen says, "There isn't much privacy. My mother and two daughters share the same bedroom. I know it is difficult for my mother when my daughters make a lot of noise. It's never quiet in a big family! And when my husband and I argue, my mother always knows!"

CHECK YOUR UNDERSTANDING

Ⓐ Read the article again. What is the main idea of the article? Circle the letter.

a. It is becoming more common for families in the U.S. to live together.

b. Housing is expensive.

c. Ya-Wen's family takes care of one another.

B **Match the sentences with the same meaning.**

1. __d__ In many cultures, a traditional family has four generations living under one roof.

2. ____ There are benefits to living with a big family.

3. ____ My husband and I argue.

4. ____ My mother and daughter share the same bedroom.

5. ____ There isn't much privacy.

a. We don't agree with each other and get angry.

b. There are good things about living in a three- or four-generation household.

c. There are few chances to be alone.

d. In the past, family members lived together in the same home.

e. They sleep in the same room.

C **Answer the questions with information from the article.**

1. What are three benefits of families living together?

_____

_____

_____

2. What are two ways that living together can be difficult?

_____

_____

D **MAKE IT PERSONAL. Do you want to live in a three- or four-generation household? Explain why or why not.**

_____

_____

_____

A Complete the sentences. Underline the correct words.

1. Lanh works in a Vietnamese restaurant and Trinh **do / does**, too.

2. My parents speak French and I **do / does**, too.

3. Mayra's fiancé has family in Mexico and Mayra **do / does**, too.

4. Sung-Li doesn't live in San Francisco and her brother **don't / doesn't**, either.

5. Mr. Martinez works at night and his sons **do / does**, too.

6. Oskar and Karen don't have a car and their neighbors **don't / doesn't**, either.

7. Our friends don't work downtown and we **don't / doesn't**, either.

8. I don't live in a big apartment and my co-worker **don't / doesn't**, either.

B Combine the sentences. Use *do, too; does, too; don't, either;* or *doesn't, either.*

1. Jason and I live in Miami. Our sister lives in Miami.

   Jason and I live in Miami and our sister does, too.

2. Yolanda works for a computer company. Her brother-in-law works for a computer company.

   _____

3. Our parents don't live near a park. We don't live near a park.

   _____

4. Edward works from 8:00 to 5:00. His daughters work from 8:00 to 5:00.

   _____

5. Henri doesn't have any sisters. I don't have any sisters.

   _____

6. I don't work on Sundays. My husband doesn't work on Sundays.

   _____

C 🔘 Play track 6. Listen to the conversation. Complete the sentences about the people. Use *do, too; does, too; don't, either;* or *doesn't, either.*

1. Phil has _____ and Ben _____.

2. Phil _____ in Las Vegas and Ben _____.

3. Phil works for a _____ and Ben _____.

4. Phil's parents don't _____ in Las Vegas and Ben's parents _____

5. Phil's _____ live in Ohio and Ben's parents _____.

D Look at five members of the Carlson family. How are the people similar? Complete the sentences. Use the correct verb (plus preposition, if needed) and *do, too; does, too; don't, either;* or *doesn't, either.*

| Alan, school principal, Atlanta | Brian, nurse, Atlanta | Carol, teacher, Atlanta | Deborah, doctor, Memphis | Angela, bus driver, Memphis |

1. Carol _____*lives in*_____ Atlanta and Alan and Brian _____*do, too*_____.

2. Alan _____ curly hair and Carol _____.

3. Angela _____ a hospital and Carol _____.

4. Carol and Deborah _____ brown hair and Brian _____.

5. Brian _____ curly hair and Deborah _____.

6. Alan _____ a moustache and Brian _____.

7. Angela _____ straight hair and Alan _____.

8. Carol _____ Memphis and Brian _____.

A Look at the pictures. Write the words.

1. <u>l e t t e r</u>

2. _<u>a</u>_ _<u>i</u>_ _ _<u>u</u>_ _ _

3. <u>l</u> _ <u>r</u> _ <u>e</u> _ <u>n</u> _ _ _ <u>o</u> _ <u>e</u>

4. _ <u>o</u> _ _ <u>a</u> _ _

5. _ _ <u>c</u> _ <u>g</u> _

B Look at the charts of some post office mailing services. Then read the sentences and correct the information.

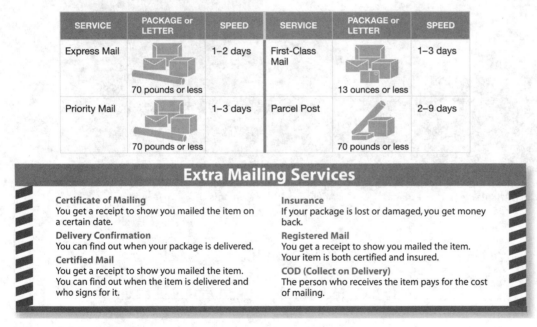

SERVICE	PACKAGE or LETTER	SPEED	SERVICE	PACKAGE or LETTER	SPEED
Express Mail	70 pounds or less	1–2 days	First-Class Mail	13 ounces or less	1–3 days
Priority Mail	70 pounds or less	1–3 days	Parcel Post	70 pounds or less	2–9 days

Extra Mailing Services

Certificate of Mailing
You get a receipt to show you mailed the item on a certain date.

Delivery Confirmation
You can find out when your package is delivered.

Certified Mail
You get a receipt to show you mailed the item. You can find out when the item is delivered and who signs for it.

Insurance
If your package is lost or damaged, you get money back.

Registered Mail
You get a receipt to show you mailed the item. Your item is both certified and insured.

COD (Collect on Delivery)
The person who receives the item pays for the cost of mailing.

1. You can send a postcard by ~~Parcel Post.~~ *First-Class Mail*

2. It takes 2–9 days for an Express Mail letter to arrive.

3. You can send a 90-pound package by Priority Mail.

4. You can send a 12-ounce mailing tube by First-Class Mail.

5. With Certified Mail, the person you send the item to pays the cost of mailing.

6. With Delivery Confirmation, you get money back if the package is lost.

C 💿 Play track 7. Listen to the conversation. Answer the questions.

1. What does the customer want to mail?

   a. a letter   b. a package   c. a large envelope

2. How does the customer send it?

   a. First Class   b. Parcel Post   c. Priority Mail

3. What extra mailing service does the customer want?

   a. Insurance   b. Certified Mail   c. Delivery Confirmation

D Read what each customer wants. Look at the mailing services charts in Exercise B on page 22. What are the best services for each customer?

Jun needs to mail a large envelope. It needs to arrive in three days. The package weighs 10 ounces. He wants a receipt to show he mailed it. He also wants to know when it was delivered and who signed for it.

Mailing services: _____

Angela needs to mail a package. The package weighs 25 pounds. It needs to arrive in three days. She wants to get her money back if the package is lost.

Mailing services: _____

E MAKE IT PERSONAL. Look at the mailing services charts on page 22 again. Think about something that you need to mail. How do you want to send it? Do you need any extra services?

Type of mail: _____ Service: _____

Extra services: _____

A Complete the sentences. Write *do* or *does*.

1. __Do__ you work in an office?

2. _____ Mr. Johnson stay late at work?

3. _____ they send e-mail to their families every week?

4. _____ he call his mother every day?

5. _____ Benji and his wife have a big family?

6. _____ your brother live near you?

B Complete the conversations. Write *Yes / No* questions and short answers.

1. **A:** __Does__ your nephew __live__ in the United States?

   B: Yes, __he does__. My nephew lives here in Phoenix.

2. **A:** _____ you _____ a brother?

   B: No, _____. I have three sisters.

3. **A:** _____ Nelly _____ packages to her family in Puerto Rico?

   B: Yes, _____. She mails packages to her family every month.

4. **A:** _____ Leandro _____ with his cousins?

   B: Yes, _____. Leandro lives with his cousins in Chicago.

5. **A:** _____ the grandchildren _____ their grandparents every weekend?

   B: No, _____. They visit their grandparents once a month.

6. **A:** _____ you and your sister _____ in touch with your aunt?

   B: Yes, _____. We keep in touch with her by phone and e-mail.

C Unscramble the sentences. Write information questions.

1. (do / where / live / you) _Where do you live?_ _____

2. (brothers and sisters / you / how many / do / have) _____

   _____

3. (call / your best friend / you / do / how often) _____

   _____

4. (you / study English / do / where) _____

5. (visit / you / when / your family / do) _____

6. (do / with your family / how / keep in touch / you) _____

   _____

D Read the answers. Write information questions about the underlined information. Use *Which, When, Where, How, How many,* or *How often*.

1. **A:** _Where does Franco live?_ _____

   B: Franco lives <u>near the bus station</u>.

2. **A:** _____

   B: Dorothea works <u>at night</u>.

3. **A:** _____

   B: I have <u>ten</u> cousins.

4. **A:** _____

   B: Jackie e-mails her family <u>every day</u>.

5. **A:** _____

   B: My youngest daughter, Hey-Jin, lives in <u>San Diego</u>.

6. **A:** _____

   B: Mr. and Mrs. Shuh keep in touch with their son <u>by phone</u>.

E MAKE IT PERSONAL. Answer the questions in Exercise C with your own information.

A Look at the pictures. Write the names of the clothes that match the numbers. Use the words in the box.

boots	coat	gloves	~~jacket~~	jeans
raincoat	scarf	sweatshirt	windbreaker	

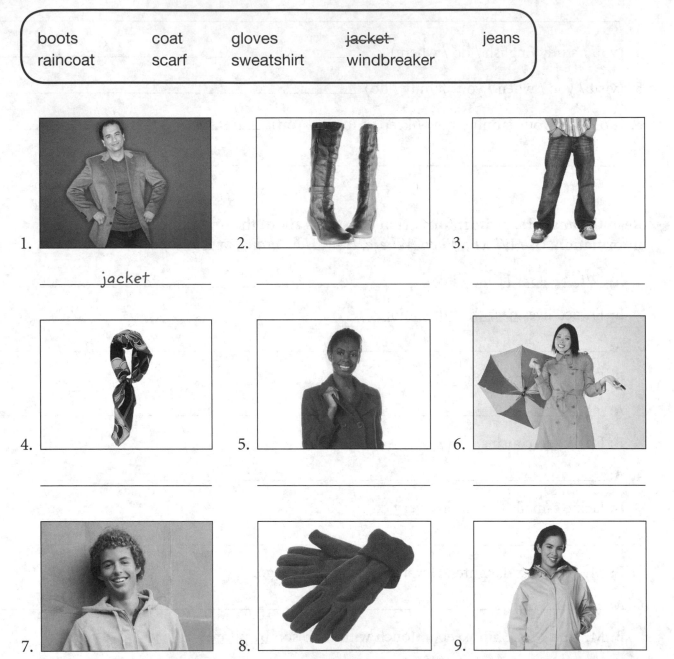

1. _____ *jacket* _____

2. _____

3. _____

4. _____

5. _____

6. _____

7. _____

8. _____

9. _____

B Look at the chart. Which word doesn't belong? Cross out the item of clothing that does not match each material.

Material	Clothing		
leather	jacket	boots	~~sweatshirt~~
wool	windbreaker	coat	scarf
fleece	gloves	sweatshirt	raincoat
denim	jeans	jacket	boots
corduroy	jacket	pants	scarf
vinyl	raincoat	boots	jeans

C Look at the pictures. What are the people wearing? Write the clothing.

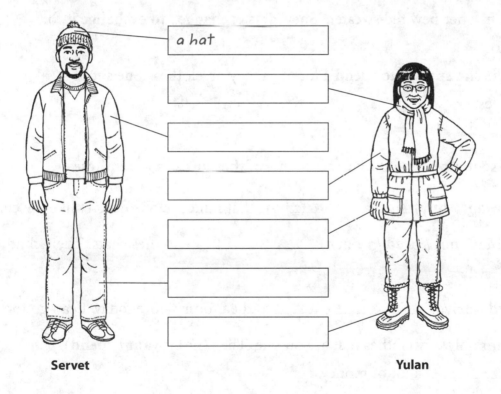

a hat

Servet   Yulan

D MAKE IT PERSONAL. What clothing are you wearing today? Write a list. Include the color and material.

_____

_____

A Complete the sentences. Circle the correct answers.

1. Let's go to the shoe store. I need **buy /(to buy)** some new shirts for work.

2. I can't buy a new coat today. I need **save / to save** some money first.

3. Shopmart has a big sale on jeans but I didn't buy anything. I couldn't **find / to find** my size.

4. Naomi wants **return / to return** her new skirt. She doesn't like it.

5. Oscar needs **leave / to leave** class at 3:00. He has a doctor's appointment.

6. Luz doesn't like her new red sweater. She wants **exchange / to exchange** it for another color.

7. Mrs. Silva doesn't **spend / to spend** a lot of money on clothes. She shops at clearance sales.

B Complete the sentences. Use the correct forms of the words in parentheses.

1. Tien (**not / want / buy**) _doesn't want to buy_ that raincoat. She doesn't like the color.

2. Olivia and Max (**not / need / return**) _____ these hats. Their children like them.

3. I (**not / need / drive**) _____ to the grocery store today. I can go tomorrow.

4. Julia and Sam only buy clothes that are on sale. They (**not / want / spend**) _____ a lot of money.

5. I (**not / want / go**) _____ to the shoe store with you. I don't need any shoes.

6. Mi-Young (**not / want / exchange**) _____ this silk scarf. She wants her money back.

C Look at the picture. Write a sentence about what each customer wants or needs to do. Use *need* or *want* + an infinitive. There may be more than one correct answer.

Charles   Maria   Pietro   Tai-Ling   Joe

Charles needs to exchange a jacket.

_____

_____

_____

_____

D MAKE IT PERSONAL. What do you need or want to do today? Write three true sentences.

_____

_____

_____

A Look at the receipts. Calculate the change for each sale.

1.
```
CLOTHESMART

09/07/10
Women's Wear
1 corduroy jacket    $49.99
Discount 20%        -  9.99
Subtotal              40.00
Sales Tax 6%           2.40
Total                $42.40
CASH                  50.00
Change              $ 7.60
```

2.
```
CLOTHESMART

09/17/10
Men's Shoe Department
1 pair leather boots  $69.99
Discount 30%          -21.00
Subtotal               48.99
Sales Tax 7%            3.43
Total                 $52.42
CASH                   60.00
Change              _____
```

3.
```
CLOTHESMART

09/18/10
Boys Active Wear
1 pair denim jeans   $25.95
Discount 15%        -  3.89
Subtotal              22.06
Sales Tax 8%           1.76
Total                $23.82
CASH                  40.00
Change              _____
```

4.
```
CLOTHESMART

10/15/10
Women's Outerwear
1 pair fleece gloves $16.99
Discount 20%        -  3.40
Subtotal              13.59
Sales Tax 5%            .68
Total                $14.27
CASH                  20.00
Change              _____
```

B Look at the receipts in Exercise A. Answer the questions.

1. What is the name of the store on the receipts? ____ClothesMart____

2. How much is the jacket after the discount and before tax? _____

3. What is the date on the receipt for the jacket? _____

4. How much are the boots after tax? _____

5. What is the amount of the discount on the jeans? _____

6. How much money does the customer give the cashier for the gloves? _____

C Read the store ad. Circle the clothing items that are on sale.

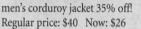

Cole's Department Store
Thursday, October 28th – Sunday, October 31st

Big Fall Sale!

All men's and women's outerwear on sale!

Come see our low prices on clothes for children and teens!

women's nylon windbreaker 25% off!
Regular price: $25   Now: $18.75

men's corduroy jacket 35% off!
Regular price: $40   Now: $26

women's vinyl raincoat 30% off!
Regular price: $30   Now: $21

children's cotton sweatshirt
Everyday low price: $15.00

D Read the store ad in Exercise C again. Then check the receipts below. One receipt is correct. Three receipts have a mistake. Circle the mistakes.

1.
Cole's Department Store

10/28/10	
Women's Outerwear	
1 windbreaker	$25.00
Discount 10%	- 2.50
Subtotal	22.50
Sales Tax 8%	1.80
Total	$24.30
Cash	25.00
Change	.70

2.
Cole's Department Store

10/31/10	
Men's Outerwear	
1 jacket	$40.00
Discount 35%	-14.00
Subtotal	26.00
Sales Tax 8%	2.08
Total	$28.08
Cash	30.00
Change	1.92

3.
Cole's Department Store

10/30/10	
Women's Outerwear	
1 raincoat	$30.00
Discount 20%	- 6.00
Subtotal	24.00
Sales Tax 8%	1.92
Total	$25.92
Cash	25.92
Change	.00

4.
Cole's Department Store

10/29/10	
Children's Outerwear	
1 sweatshirt	$25.00
Sales Tax 8%	2.00
Total	$27.00
Cash	30.00
Change	3.00

A Complete the e-mail message. Use the correct forms of *be going to* and the verbs. Use contractions if possible.

Hi Beatriz,

I'm happy you *'re going to visit* us this weekend! Please come on Sunday because our family
 _____
 1. visit
 _____ busy on Saturday. We _____ some spring cleaning.
 2. be   **3. do**
Fernando _____ the laundry, and I _____ the bathroom. Our kids, José
                   4. do   **5. clean**
and Manny _____ their rooms. In the afternoon, my mother-in-law _____
                        6. clean   **7. take**
the kids to the movies. Fernando and I _____ the living room and wash the floors.
                                                          8. paint
The house _____ beautiful when you see it on Sunday!
                   9. look

See you soon!

Evelia

B Read the e-mail message in Exercise A again. Then read the sentences. Correct the mistakes. Use the correct form of *be going to*. Use contractions if possible.

1. Evelia is going to relax on Saturday.

    Evelia isn't going to relax on Saturday. She's going to be busy.

2. Beatriz is going to visit on Saturday.

    _____

3. The children are going to clean the bathroom.

    _____

4. Evelia's mother-in-law is going to take Fernando to a movie.

    _____

5. Fernando and Evelia are going to paint the bedroom.

    _____

6. Fernando and Evelia are going to wash the floors on Sunday.

    _____

C   🎧 **Play track 8. Listen to the conversation. Write the missing words. Use contractions if possible.**

Irene: I can't wait for Jeff's birthday party tonight! Do I need to bring anything?

Cindy: Well, let's see. Scott _____ some ice cream on his way home from work.

        Alex and Nina _____ pizza and soda. I _____ a cake.

Irene: Did you remember the decorations?

Cindy: Yes. My sister _____ balloons and party games.

Irene: Cake, ice cream, pizza, games . . . sounds like it _____ a fun party!

Cindy: Oh no! I need to go to the store.

Irene: Why?

Cindy: I forgot something very important. I forgot to buy Jeff's birthday present!

D   **Read the class poll. What are the students going to do after class? Write sentences about their plans. Use the correct forms of *being going to*.**

Class Poll: What are you going to do after English class?

Student	Activity	Student	Activity
Alfonso	hang out with friends	Ana	hang out with friends
Monique	clean her house	Javier	get lunch at a deli
Ji-Su	cook lunch for her kids	Bernard	go home and relax
James	go home and relax		

1. Monique _____

2. Alfonso and Ana _____

3. Ji-Su _____

4. James and Bernard _____

5. Javier _____

READ

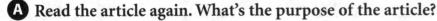 **Play track 9. Listen. Read the article.**

Top 5 Shopping Secrets
A smart shopper's guide to saving money

These days, prices are going up. It takes more money to pay for things like food and clothing. But there are ways that you can save money. Here are five tips to help you spend less on the things you need.

1. Look for clearance sales. Stores give big discounts at the end of each season. They need to make room for new products. Shop for winter coats and hats in March. Shop for summer shorts and swimsuits in July. You'll find discounts of 50 percent to 85 percent off regular prices.

2. Buy after big holidays. Stores have sales after the Thanksgiving and Christmas holidays. These holidays are the best times to buy toys, movies, music, and electronic items. Check the Sunday newspaper for sale ads.

3. Watch for back-to-school sales in August. Many stores have big sales in August. At this time, parents are getting their children ready for the new school year. Stores give discounts on clothes, shoes, and school supplies.

4. Use coupons. Coupons are a popular way to save on food and household items. Many grocery stores will double the amount of your coupons. This means that a coupon for fifty cents off will save you one dollar. Many department stores also offer coupons. These coupons give you a discount, such as 20 percent off one item. You can find coupons in newspapers, magazines, store ads, and also online.

5. Check prices online. Prices on the Internet are often lower than prices at regular stores. This is especially true for electronic items, computers, airline tickets, books, and music. It is always a good idea to check prices on the Internet before you buy an item in a store.

CHECK YOUR UNDERSTANDING

A **Read the article again. What's the purpose of the article?**

a. To compare prices at different stores.

b. To help the reader save money.

c. To recommend Internet stores.

B Read how the shoppers save money. Write the number of the tip in the article that matches each person.

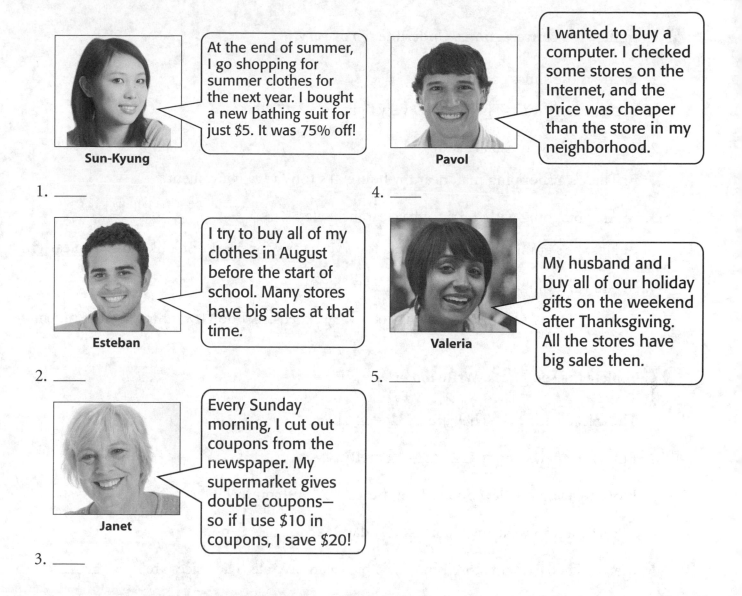

At the end of summer, I go shopping for summer clothes for the next year. I bought a new bathing suit for just $5. It was 75% off!

Sun-Kyung

1. ___

I wanted to buy a computer. I checked some stores on the Internet, and the price was cheaper than the store in my neighborhood.

Pavol

4. ___

I try to buy all of my clothes in August before the start of school. Many stores have big sales at that time.

Esteban

2. ___

My husband and I buy all of our holiday gifts on the weekend after Thanksgiving. All the stores have big sales then.

Valeria

5. ___

Every Sunday morning, I cut out coupons from the newspaper. My supermarket gives double coupons— so if I use $10 in coupons, I save $20!

Janet

3. ___

C MAKE IT PERSONAL. How do you save money when you shop? Do you use any of the tips in the article?

I use coupons at the supermarket.

_____

_____

_____

A Complete the conversations. Underline *too* or *very*.

1. **A:** Are those shoes comfortable?

   B: No. I can't walk. They're **too** / **very** tight.

2. **A:** Where do you usually shop?

   B: There's a shopping mall near my house. It's **too** / **very** convenient.

3. **A:** Are you going with Terri to the clearance sale?

   B: No. She's going at 7:00 A.M. That's **too** / **very** early for me. I don't like to get up early!

4. **A:** Are you going to get the denim jacket?

   B: No. It's **too** / **very** pretty, but it's **too** / **very** expensive. I don't want to pay that much.

B Complete the sentences. Write *too* or *very*.

1. These jeans don't fit. They are _____*too*_____ big.

2. I like your new coat. It's _____ pretty.

3. I love wearing my new boots. They are _____ comfortable.

4. I don't want to wear my wool jacket today. It's _____ hot.

5. Merritt's department store is having a big clearance sale. The prices are _____ low.

6. The weather is _____ good today. It's not _____ hot or cold.

C Play track 10. Listen to the conversations. Why does each person return the clothing item? Circle the correct answer.

1. a. The pants are too short.   b. The pants are too big.

2. a. There's a hole in the jacket.   b. The jacket is too tight.

3. a. The shirt is too loose.   b. A seam is ripped.

4. a. A button is missing.   b. It's too big.

5. a. The boots are too big.   b. The boots are too tight.

D Look at the picture. Matt and Jake are new employees. They have some problems with their uniforms. What's wrong with each piece of clothing? Write six sentences.

1. *The hat is too small.*

2.

3.

4.

5.

6.

7.

8.

Unit 4: Small Talk

Lesson 1: Vocabulary

A Look at the pictures. Write the activities. Use the words in the box.

> go dancing   ~~go fishing~~   go for a bike ride   go for a walk
> go hiking   go out to eat   go shopping   go swimming

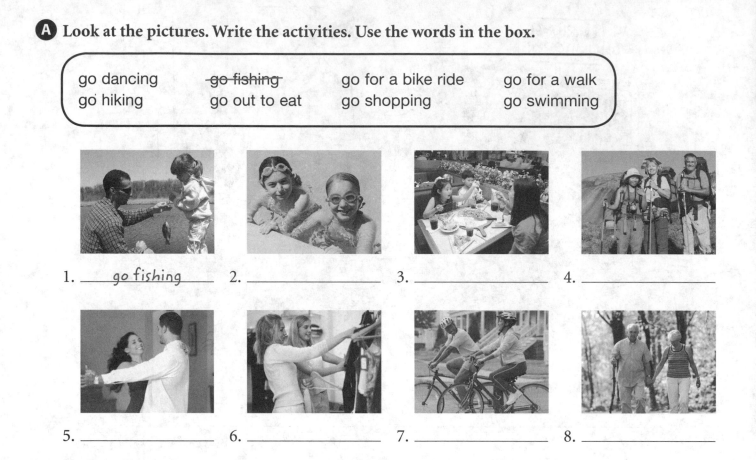

1. ___go fishing___   2. _____   3. _____   4. _____

5. _____   6. _____   7. _____   8. _____

B WORD PLAY. Complete the chart. Write the words in the correct columns.

> ~~beach~~   bike ride   dancing   fishing
> jogging   park   walk   zoo

go	go to the	go for a
	beach	

C Look at the pictures and complete the paragraph. Write the activities from the pictures.

My family is very active. We like to spend our free time outdoors. Some weekends, we go to the park. My wife and I like to _____ and our children _____. Some weekends, we _____ in the mountains. The view from the top is beautiful! We also like to _____. We all love being near the water. My wife and kids love to _____, and I like to _____. The only problem is that I never catch any fish!

D MAKE IT PERSONAL. Answer the questions about your own free-time activities.

1. What is your favorite outdoor activity? _____

2. What is your favorite indoor activity? _____

A Complete the conversations. Underline the correct words.

1. **A:** Is Martin doing well in his guitar class?

   B: No, he's not. He is <u>always</u> / **never** late for class, and he **never** / **always** practices.

2. **A:** My kids and I go for a bike ride every weekend.

   B: You're lucky. I **hardly ever** / **often** go for a bike ride. I'm too busy.

3. **A:** I'll make the kids a snack.

   B: Good idea. They're **usually** / **never** hungry after school.

4. **A:** What do you do in your free time?

   B: Well, I **sometimes** / **never** go to the movies with my friends. There's a great theater downtown.

5. **A:** My kids love to go to the zoo.

   B: My kids do, too. We **sometimes** / **hardly ever** spend the whole day there.

B Write sentences. Put the words in the correct order.

1. we / go fishing / usually / on Sundays

   We usually go fishing on Sundays.

2. always / goes dancing / on Saturday nights / Benita

   _____

3. go out to eat / never / my wife and I

   _____

4. in the summer / Ben and Janice / go hiking / often

   _____

5. my father / goes shopping / hardly ever

   _____

C Write questions with *How often*. Use the words in parentheses.

1. (the children / go swimming) <u>How often do the children go swimming?</u>

2. (the family / go for a bike ride) _____

3. (Dolores / work late) _____

4. (Alfredo and Dolores / go out to eat) _____

5. (the family / visit Grandma) _____

D Look at the Lozado family's calendar. Then answer the questions in Exercise C with complete sentences. There may be more than one correct answer.

Lozado Family Calendar   February

Sun.	Mon.	Tue.	Wed.	Thu.	Fri.	Sat.
1 Paco and Isabel—swimming	2 bike ride	3 Dolores works late	4	5 Alfredo—ESL class	6 visit Grandma	7 go out to eat
8 Alfredo—soccer in the park	9 bike ride	10 Paco and Isabel—go to the park	11	12 Alfredo—ESL class	13	14 Alfredo and Dolores—dancing
15 Alfredo—soccer in the park	16 bike ride	17 Paco and Isabel—go to the park	18	19 Alfredo—ESL class	20 visit Grandma	21
22 29	23 bike ride	24 Dolores works late	25	26 Alfredo—ESL class	27	28 Alfredo and Dolores—dancing

1. <u>The children go swimming once a month.</u>

2. _____

3. _____

4. _____

5. _____

A Look at the calendar. Complete the sentences about the events.

R osemont C ommunity C enter						January
Sunday	Monday	Tuesday	Wednesday	Thursday	Friday	Saturday
			1 computer class 1:00–3:00 P.M.	2 ESL class 9:00 A.M.– 12:00 P.M.	3 painting class 11:00 A.M.– 1:00 P.M.	4 Dance Club 8:00–10:00 P.M.
5 Bike Club 8:00–11:00 A.M.	6 cooking class 6:30–8:30 P.M.	7 ESL class 9:00 A.M.– 12:00 P.M.	8 computer class 1:00–3:00 P.M.	9 ESL class 9:00 A.M.– 12:00 P.M.	10 painting class 11:00 A.M.– 1:00 P.M.	11 Movie Club 8:00–10:00 P.M.
12	13 cooking class 6:30–8:30 P.M.	14 ESL class 9:00 A.M.– 12:00 P.M.	15 computer class 1:00–3:00 P.M.	16 ESL class 9:00 A.M.– 12:00 P.M.	17 painting class 11:00 A.M.– 1:00 P.M.	18 Dance Club 8:00–10:00 P.M.
19	20 cooking class 6:30–8:30 P.M.	21 ESL class 9:00 A.M.– 12:00 P.M.	22 computer class 1:00–3:00 P.M.	23 ESL class 9:00 A.M.– 12:00 P.M.	24 painting class 11:00 A.M.– 1:00 P.M.	25 Movie Club 8:00–10:00 P.M.
26	27 cooking class 6:30–8:30 P.M.	28 ESL class 9:00 A.M.– 12:00 P.M.	29 computer class 1:00–3:00 P.M.	30 ESL class 9:00 A.M.– 12:00 P.M.	31 painting class 11:00 A.M.– 1:00 P.M.	

1. The ESL class meets on _Tuesdays and Thursdays_ from _9:00_ A.M. to _12:00_ P.M.

2. The cooking class meets every _____ at _____ P.M.

3. The Dance Club meets on the first and third _____ of the month from

    _____ to _____ P.M.

4. The painting class starts at _____ A.M. and ends at _____ P.M.

B Look at the calendar in Exercise A again. Answer the questions.

1. When does the Bike Club meet? _____

2. When does the Movie Club meet? _____

3. What time does the computer class start? _____

C 🎵 **Play track 11. Listen to the conversations. When is each event?**

1. When is the dance class?
   a. the first Monday of the month from 7:00 to 9:00 P.M.
   b. the first and third Monday of the month from 7:00 to 9:00 P.M.

2. When is the English class?
   a. on Tuesdays and Thursdays from 5:30 to 7:00 P.M.
   b. on Tuesdays and Thursdays from 7:00 to 8:00 P.M.

3. When is the swimming class?
   a. on Wednesdays from 4:00 to 6:00 P.M.
   b. on Mondays and Wednesdays from 4:00 to 6:00 P.M.

4. When does the Walking Club meet?
   a. on Sundays from 7:00 to 8:00 A.M.
   b. on Sundays from 7:00 to 8:00 P.M.

5. When is the Movie Night?
   a. on Saturdays at 7:30 P.M.
   b. on Sundays at 7:30 P.M.

D **Complete the calendar with events from Exercise C. Write the names and the times of the events.**

Greenville October
Community Center Calendar

Sunday	Monday	Tuesday	Wednesday	Thursday	Friday	Saturday
		1	2	3	4	5
6	7	8 Columbus Day	9	10	11	12
13	14	15	16	17	18	19
20	21	22	23	24	25	26
27	28	29	30	31 Halloween		

A Complete the sentences. Use the correct form of the verbs in parentheses and an infinitive.

1. I (**like / take**) _____like to take_____ my daughter to the park.

2. The children (**not like / study**) _____ after school.

3. My husband (**hate / iron**) _____ the clothes.

4. Alak and Dao (**like / go**) _____ to concerts.

5. Sonya (**not like / stay home**) _____ on the weekends.

6. Mr. Patel (**like / go**) _____ for bike rides on Sundays.

7. Ivan (**hate / get up**) _____ early on Mondays.

8. Lara (**not like / swim**) _____ at the beach.

B Look at the information in the chart. Then complete each sentence. Use the correct form of the verb and an infinitive.

	exercise	study	cook	get up early
Jackie	like	love	doesn't like	doesn't like
Jun	love	like	hate	like
Carmen	hate	doesn't like	love	like
Jean Paul	doesn't like	love	doesn't like	love

1. Jackie _____likes to_____ exercise.

2. Jun and Carmen _____ get up early.

3. Jackie and Jean Paul _____ study.

4. Jackie and Jean Paul _____ cook.

5. Carmen _____ study.

6. Jean Paul _____ exercise.

7. Jun _____ cook.

8. Jean Paul _____ get up early.

C 🔘 **Play track 12. Listen to the conversations. Check (✓) the people who like each activity.**

1.

	Rick	Angie
go hiking		
go to the beach		

2.

	Fred	Liz
eat Italian food		
go dancing		

D **Look at Mathew's web page. What does Mathew like and dislike? Write six sentences with *love* and *hate* plus infinitives.**

MY PAGE   HOME   MY PROFILE   MY PHOTOS   MY FRIENDS

About Me

Name: Mathew
Location: Fort Worth, Texas

Things I love: fishing
swimming
doing karate
playing video games
walking my dog

Things I hate: getting up early
cooking
shopping

1. _____
2. _____
3. _____
4. _____
5. _____
6. _____

READ

Play track 13. Listen. Read the letters from a newspaper advice column.

Dear Kate
Advice for
Life

Dear Kate,

I have an American friend at work. She invited me to have dinner at her home. I really want to go and meet her family, but I'm a little nervous. I don't know a lot about American culture. I'm afraid of making a mistake! Help!
Lorette from Honduras

Dear Lorette,

Don't worry. I'm sure that you're going to have a great time! Here are a few tips.

It is important to be on time for dinner. Don't arrive more than fifteen minutes late.

It is polite to bring a small, inexpensive gift when you visit someone's home. For example, you can bring flowers, a dessert, or a box of chocolates. You could also give your friend something from your country. Spend about five dollars. An expensive gift may embarrass your friend.

Americans are usually informal at meals. Here are a few rules for the table. In many homes, dishes of food are passed around the table. You should take only the amount of food you want to eat. It's OK to take more later. Don't reach across the table to get something. Ask someone to pass it to you. When everyone has food, your friend will invite everyone to eat. For example, she may say "Please eat," or "Let's eat." Wait until someone else begins eating to be sure.

Most important, relax and enjoy the dinner!
Kate

CHECK YOUR UNDERSTANDING

Ⓐ What is the topic of both letters in the advice column? Circle the answer.

a. Information about American food

b. Advice about giving gifts

c. Rude and polite behavior in the U.S.

B Read the advice column again. Complete each sentence with Kate's advice.

1. Don't arrive more than _____ minutes late for a dinner invitation.

2. It's polite to bring a _____ when you visit someone's home.

3. Don't give your friend an _____. It may embarrass her.

4. If you need to get something across the table, ask someone to _____.

5. Before you start eating, wait for your friend to say, " _____."

C Read the statements. According to Kate's advice, which actions are rude in the United States? Which actions are polite? Circle *Rude* or *Polite*.

1. The dinner starts at 6:00. Edith arrives at 6:30. **Rude** **Polite**

2. Edith gives her friend a box of chocolates. **Rude** **Polite**

3. Edith begins eating before the other people are ready to eat. **Rude** **Polite**

4. Edith finishes the food on her plate and asks for more. **Rude** **Polite**

5. Edith asks someone to pass the salt. **Rude** **Polite**

D MAKE IT PERSONAL. Imagine you are visiting someone's home in your own country. What is polite? What is rude?

In my country, it is polite to take off your shoes when
you visit someone's home.

_____

_____

A Complete the sentences. Use the infinitive forms of the verbs in the box.

~~cook~~   exercise   get up   meet   pay   take

1. We have plans to eat out tonight. I don't have __to cook__ dinner.

2. Ramadan has _____ his new boss at 9:00 in the morning.

3. Lian wants to be healthy. She has _____ every day.

4. Roger drives his children to school. They don't have _____ the bus.

5. Parking is free on holidays. Drivers don't have _____ for parking.

6. Jalana has _____ early during the week. She starts work at 6:30 A.M.

B Complete the conversation. Use the correct forms of *have to* and the words.

Chuck: Guess what? I got free tickets to the zoo. Do you and the kids want to go

this Saturday?

Melinda: That sounds like fun, but I ___have to work___ this Saturday.
                                          1. work

Chuck: Oh. Do you have any plans on Sunday?

Melinda: Well, I don't, but Barry _____ to his
                                        2. go

guitar class. And Tina _____ in a soccer game. How about next Saturday?
                        3. play

I _____ that day.
  4. not work

Chuck: Hmm. Actually, I _____ my mother to a wedding. Can you go
                               5. take
on Sunday?

Melinda: No, Sunday's not good. I _____ my sister. She's moving to a
                                      6. help
new apartment.

Chuck: Oh, well. Too bad.

C Read the invitations from Sandra's friends. Then look at Sandra's calendar. Can Sandra accept the invitations? Write Sandra's answers.

Sandra

	Sandra's Calendar			June 4-10		
Sunday	**Monday**	**Tuesday**	**Wednesday**	**Thursday**	**Friday**	**Saturday**
4 1:00 P.M. lunch with Mom and Dad	5 7:00 A.M. – 3:00 P.M. Work	6 7:00 A.M. – 3:00 P.M. Work 6:00 – 8:00 P.M. ESL class	7 7:00 A.M. – 3:00 P.M. Work 3:45 P.M. dentist	8 7:00 A.M. – 3:00 P.M. Work 6:00 – 8:00 P.M. ESL class	9 7:00 A.M. – 3:00 P.M. Work 3:30 P.M. Meet with Miguel's teacher	10 9:00 –11:00 A.M. computer class 1:00 P.M. Miguel's birthday party

Can you go for a bike ride on Saturday morning?

1.

Sorry, I can't. I have to go to my

computer class.

I'm going to the beach on Saturday at around 1:00. Do you want to come?

4.

Do you want to watch a video on Monday night?

2.

Do you want to get some lunch on Sunday afternoon?

5.

Can you go for a walk on Thursday evening—at around 6:00?

3.

Lesson 1: Vocabulary

A Complete the sentences. Match the beginnings and endings.

1. __c__ Don't use the bathroom because

2. ____ I can't get my mail because

3. ____ I can't cook dinner because

4. ____ My key won't open the door because

5. ____ I have to go to a laundromat because

a. the washing machine is broken.

b. the lock is broken.

c. the toilet is clogged.

d. the mailbox is broken.

e. the stove isn't working.

B Complete the conversations. Use the words in the box.

> leaking   no heat   no hot water
> ~~stuck~~   working

1. **A:** It's hot in here. Could you open the window?

   B: I can't. It's _____ stuck _____.

2. **A:** It's very cold in the house.

   B: I know. There's _____.

3. **A:** There's water on the bedroom floor.

   B: I saw that. The ceiling is _____.

4. **A:** You can't wash the dishes.

   B: Why not?

   A: There's _____.

5. **A:** I'm going to the laundromat.

   B: Why? Is there something wrong with the washing machine?

   A: Yes. It's not _____.

C Look at the pictures. What are the problems? Write sentences.

1. ___The door is stuck.___

2. _____

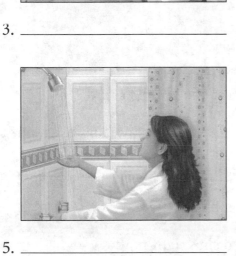

3. _____

4. _____

5. _____

6. _____

D MAKE IT PERSONAL. Do you have any problems in your home?
What are they?

___The window in my bathroom is stuck.___

_____

_____

A Complete the sentences. Underline the correct word.

1. The plumber **is** / **are** fixing the sink.

2. I **are** / **am** calling an electrician to fix the lights.

3. Mr. and Mrs. Duran **is** / **are** going shopping for a new washing machine.

4. The building manager **is** / **are** buying a new stove for our apartment.

5. Two faucets in the house **is** / **are** leaking.

6. You **am** / **are** using all the hot water. Don't take long showers!

7. You can cook now. The oven **is** / **are** working.

B Complete the sentences. Use the present continuous forms of the verbs. Use contractions when possible.

1. Elian _____*is painting*_____ the kitchen.
   paint

2. I think we need a new toilet. Juan _____ to the plumber now.
   talk

3. Marek _____ an electrician. He _____ the building manager.
   not call   **call**

4. I _____ the building manager about the broken lock.
   e-mail

5. Salvador _____ at the ceiling, but he doesn't see the leak.
   look

6. The building manager _____ the clogged sink right now.
   not fix

7. Cha-Ram is at the hardware store. She _____ a new lock.
   buy

8. I need to dry the laundry on the balcony. The dryer _____.
   not work

9. I can't do the laundry. Someone _____ the washing machine.
   use

C Look at the picture of an apartment building. What are the people doing? What problems do you see? Write six sentences.

The dishwasher is leaking in apartment 3.

1. _____

2. _____

3. _____

4. _____

5. _____

6. _____

Lesson 4: Read apartment ads

A Read the ad. Write the full word(s) for each abbreviation.

1. _____Furnished_____   10. _____

2. _____   11. _____

3. _____   12. _____

4. _____   13. _____

5. _____   14. _____

6. _____   15. _____

7. _____   16. _____

8. _____   17. _____

9. _____   18. _____

> Furn. 2 BR, 2 BA apt. on the second
> 1   2   3 4
> fl. No elevator. Large LR and DR.
> 5   6   7
> Small EIK. Ht. and hw. not incl.
>   8   9   10   11
> W/D in bsmt. A/C. Nr. shopping and
> 12   13   14 15
> trans. Parking on street. $1,400/mo.
> 16   17
> $700 sec. dep. Available May 1.
>   18
> Call Richmond Realty
> 222-555-9876.

B Look at the ad in Exercise A. Then read the sentences. Correct the mistakes, according to the information in the ad.

1. The apartment has ~~three~~ *two* bedrooms.

2. There is no furniture in the apartment.

3. The apartment has a large eat-in kitchen.

4. Hot water is included in the rent.

5. There is no air-conditioning.

6. The apartment is near a park.

7. The security deposit is one month's rent.

C Look at the apartment ads. Then read the sentences. Write the letter of the apartment on the line.

A.
> Pine Plains. Large 1 BR, 1 BA,
> LR, EIK, W/D in bsmt.
> $925/mo.+ 1 mo. sec. dep. Util. incl.
> Available immediately.
> Call Vicky 222-555-1234.

B.
> Northside. Sunny 4 BR, 2 BA apt.
> LR, DR Nr. hospital and shopping. A/C.
> Ht. and hw. not incl. Parking for two cars.
> $2,000/mo. + $1,000 sec. dep.
> Call Ahmed 222-555-4567.

1. _B_ It has four bedrooms.

2. ____ It has one bathroom.

3. ____ There is air-conditioning.

4. ____ The security deposit is one month's rent.

5. ____ Parking is available.

6. ____ It has a dining room.

7. ____ The building has a washer and dryer.

8. ____ Utilities are not included.

D Imagine a home you want to have in the future. Write an ad for your dream home. Use abbreviations.

A Play track 14. Listen and complete the conversation. Write the words you hear.

Jackie: Hello?

Charlie: Hi, Jackie. This is Charlie at Richmond Realty. I have a nice _____ to show you.

Jackie: Great! Tell me about it.

Charlie: Well, it's really nice. There are three _____. And there's a large _____.

Jackie: How many _____ are there?

Charlie: Two.

Jackie: Is there a dining room?

Charlie: There's no dining room, but there's a big _____.

Jackie: Sounds good. How's the location? Is there a _____ nearby?

Charlie: Yes, there is. Right around the corner.

Jackie: And is the neighborhood quiet?

Charlie: Yes, it's on a very quiet street. There isn't a lot of _____.

Jackie: Wow. That sounds perfect. Can I see it today?

B Read the sentences. Correct the mistakes.

1. There ~~is~~ *are* no pets allowed in the building.

2. Are there a supermarket nearby?

3. How many bathrooms is there?

4. There isn't no bus stop near here.

5. Is there a lot of stores in the neighborhood?

6. There is three bedrooms.

Imagine you are looking for an apartment. Write questions that you would ask the landlord about the apartment. Use the words in the box.

> air-conditioning   bedrooms   bus stop   laundry room
> park   parking   shops   traffic

1. _Is there air-conditioning?_

2. _____

3. _____

4. _____

5. _____

6. _____

7. _____

8. _____

D **Imagine you looked at an apartment. Read your notes. Write sentences about the apartment.**

> ### 334 North Lincoln Street, Apt. 13
>
> **Good things about the apartment:**
> near bus stop
> three bedrooms
> laundry room in basement
> no traffic on the street
>
> **Bad things about the apartment:**
> no parking
> no air-conditioning
> no shops nearby
> no parks in the area

1. _There is no air-conditioning._

2. _____

3. _____

4. _____

5. _____

6. _____

7. _____

8. _____

READ

Play track 15. Listen. Read the newspaper advice column.

Renters' Rights
Have a problem with your landlord? Write us. We can help!

Dear Renters' Rights,
When I moved into my apartment, I paid a security deposit. Now I'm moving out, but the landlord doesn't want to give back the security deposit. That's one month's rent—$700! The apartment is clean and nothing is broken. Can the landlord keep my security deposit?
—**Viet in Tampa**

Dear Viet,
No, the landlord can't keep your security deposit if the apartment is OK. If there are problems, the landlord must send you a certified letter. In the letter, the landlord must list any problems with the apartment. If he doesn't send you a letter 30 days after you move out, he must give all of your security deposit back. That's the law in Florida.
—**Renters' Rights**

Dear Renters' Rights,
The stove is broken in my apartment. I called the landlord and he said he would fix the stove. But that was five days ago. I can't cook meals for my family. We have to eat out every night for dinner. Can I stop paying my rent until he fixes it?
—**Alejandra in Orlando**

Dear Alejandra,
Yes, you can stop paying rent. But that's not the best idea. If you don't pay the rent, your landlord can take you to court—even if he doesn't fix the stove. Court can be expensive. We recommend that you try to talk to your landlord first. Write a letter to your landlord and explain the problem. Send the letter as Certified Mail, and keep a copy for yourself.
—**Renters' Rights**

CHECK YOUR UNDERSTANDING

A **Skim the letters in the advice column. Why do people write to Renters' Rights? Circle the answer.**

a. They don't have enough money to pay their rent.

b. They want information about an apartment for rent.

c. They have problems with their landlords.

B Read the letters in the advice column again. Complete the sentences.

1. Viet's landlord doesn't want to give back his _____.

2. The landlord has to send Viet a _____ if there are problems

   with the apartment.

3. Alejandra's _____ is broken.

4. Alejandra wants to stop _____.

5. If Alejandra doesn't pay her rent, her landlord can take her to _____.

C Answer the questions. Use your own words.

1. What is Viet's problem? _____

   _____

2. What is Renters' Rights advice? _____

   _____

3. What is Alejandra's problem? _____

   _____

4. What is Renters' Rights advice? _____

   _____

D MAKE IT PERSONAL. Have you ever had a problem with a landlord?
What was it?

My sink was leaking. My landlord didn't want to fix it.

_____

_____

_____

A Look at the map. Follow the directions. Where are you? Write the name of each place.

1. Start at the hotel. Go west on Park Avenue. Turn right onto Main Street. The ___supermarket___ is on the left.

2. Start at the restaurant. Go north on Main Street. At the supermarket, turn right onto School Road. Go through one traffic light. The _____ is on the left.

3. Start at the post office. Go south on Main Street. Go through two traffic lights. The _____ is on the right.

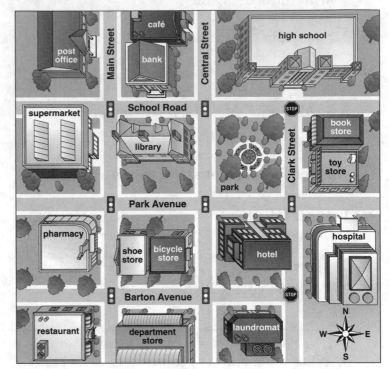

4. Start at the high school. Go south on Clark Street. At the toy store, turn right onto Park Avenue. The _____ is on the left.

5. Start at the shoe store. Go north on Main Street. Turn right onto Park Avenue. Go through one traffic light. At the next traffic light, turn left onto Clark Street. The _____ is on the left.

6. Start at the laundromat. Go east on Barton Avenue. At the stop sign, turn left. At the traffic light, turn right onto Park Avenue. The _____ is on the right.

B 🔊 **Play track 16. Listen to the conversations. Circle the directions you hear.**

1. a. At the traffic light, turn left.

   b. At the stop sign, turn right.

   c. At the stop sign, turn left.

2. a. Go straight.

   b. Turn right at this street.

   c. Go west on Fifth Street.

3. a. Go through two traffic lights.

   b. At the traffic light, turn left.

   c. Turn right at the pharmacy.

4. a. At the coffee shop, turn left.

   b. Go through two traffic lights.

   c. At the traffic light, turn right.

5. a. Go through one traffic light and turn left.

   b. At the stop sign, turn left.

   c. Turn left on Pine Street.

C 🔊 **Play track 17. Listen to the conversation. Complete the directions to the hospital.**

Directions to the hospital:

Go straight on Miller Street.

_____ two traffic lights.

Turn _____ onto Ventura Avenue.

Go through three _____ .

The hospital is on the _____ .

Unit 6: In the Past

Lesson 1: Vocabulary

A Look at the pictures. Write the names of the events. Use the words in the box.

> an anniversary party   a birthday party   a family reunion
> a funeral   a graduation party   a potluck dinner
> a retirement party   a surprise party   a wedding

1. _an anniversary party_

2. _____

3. _____

4. _____

5. _____

6. _____

7. _____

8. _____

9. _____

B **Complete the sentences with events from Exercise A.**

1. I'm going to _____a wedding_____ on Saturday. My friends Arti and Ramelan are

   getting married.

2. Bob has worked at our company for twenty-five years. Today is his last day of work.

   We're having _____ for him at lunch.

3. We're going to _____ this weekend. Everyone has to bring a different

   dish of food.

4. Myung-Hee and In-Ho Park got married on April 16, 1979. Today is April 16.

   Tonight they're having _____.

5. My grandparents are planning _____ this summer. All of my cousins,

   aunts, and uncles are going to be there.

6. Ted is fifty years old today. Ted doesn't know it, but his friends are having

   _____ for him.

7. Martin is going to _____ today. His Uncle Luis died. He was 99 years old.

8. This is Tatiana's last day of high school. Her parents are very proud. They are

   having _____ tonight.

C **Play track 18. Listen to the conversations. What kinds of events are the people attending? Write the events.**

1. _____

2. _____

3. _____

4. _____

A Complete the paragraph. Use the simple past forms of the words in parentheses.

Amy and Tom (**stay**) ___stayed___ at home yesterday. Amy (**bake**) _____ cookies

and Tom (**clean**) _____ the kitchen. They both (**wash**) _____ the dishes.

Tom (**fix**) _____ a leaking faucet and Amy (**paint**) _____ the front door. They

(**work**) _____ hard. In the evening, Amy and Tom (**want**) _____ to relax, so

they (**go**) _____ to an Italian restaurant for dinner.

B Play track 19. Listen and complete the conversation.

Rich: How was the _____?

Ann: Very nice. We all missed you.

Rich: Yeah. I was sorry I couldn't go. Who was there?

Ann: The whole family _____ up. All the aunts, uncles, and cousins.

Rich: Aunt Lucy, too?

Ann: Of course. Everyone listened to her _____. And we looked at old

photos and _____ of Grandma and Grandpa's wedding.

Rich: Oh yeah? I'm sorry I missed that!

Ann: Well, you should have come! We had a great time. We _____ and

_____.

Rich: Really? I'll definitely have to go next time!

C Look at the picture of the Park family's barbecue last weekend. What did the people do? Write sentences. Use the past tense.

1. _In-Ho and Sun-Ah danced at the barbecue._
2. _____
3. _____
4. _____
5. _____
6. _____

D MAKE IT PERSONAL. Describe an event that you attended with family or friends. When was it? What did you do?

_____
_____
_____

Lesson 4: Recognize U.S. holidays

A Read the descriptions of the U.S. holidays. Write the holidays from the box.

> Christmas Day   Columbus Day   Independence Day
> Labor Day   Martin Luther King Jr. Day Memorial Day
> New Year's Day   President's Day   Thanksgiving Day
> Veterans' Day

1. On July 4 we celebrate the birthday of the United States. _____

2. On the last Monday in May we remember people who died in wars. _____

3. On the third Monday in January we remember the life of a great African-American leader.

   _____

4. On January 1 we celebrate the first day of the year. _____

5. On the first Monday in September we have barbecues and say good-bye to summer.

   _____

6. On October 13 we celebrate a man who sailed from Europe to North America.

   _____

7. On the third Monday of February we celebrate the birthday of George Washington.

   _____

8. On November 11 we honor people who served in the U.S. military. _____

9. On the fourth Thursday of November we get together with family to eat a large meal.

   _____

10. On December 25 we decorate a tree and give gifts to family and friends.

   _____

B Look at the calendar. Write the name of each U.S. holiday from Exercise A on the correct date.

New Year's Day → January 1 (Fri.)

January 2010

Sun.	Mon.	Tue.	Wed.	Thu.	Fri.	Sat.
					1	2
3	4	5	6	7	8	9
10	11	12	13	14	15	16
17	18	19	20	21	22	23
24/31	25	26	27	28	29	30

February 2010

Sun.	Mon.	Tue.	Wed.	Thu.	Fri.	Sat.
	1	2	3	4	5	6
7	8	9	10	11	12	13
14	15	16	17	18	19	20
21	22	23	24	25	26	27
28						

March 2010

Sun.	Mon.	Tue.	Wed.	Thu.	Fri.	Sat.
	1	2	3	4	5	6
7	8	9	10	11	12	13
14	15	16	17	18	19	20
21	22	23	24	25	26	27
28	29	30	31			

April 2010

Sun.	Mon.	Tue.	Wed.	Thu.	Fri.	Sat.
				1	2	3
4	5	6	7	8	9	10
11	12	13	14	15	16	17
18	19	20	21	22	23	24
25	26	27	28	29	30	

May 2010

Sun.	Mon.	Tue.	Wed.	Thu.	Fri.	Sat.
						1
2	3	4	5	6	7	8
9	10	11	12	13	14	15
16	17	18	19	20	21	22
23/30	24/31	25	26	27	28	29

June 2010

Sun.	Mon.	Tue.	Wed.	Thu.	Fri.	Sat.
		1	2	3	4	5
6	7	8	9	10	11	12
13	14	15	16	17	18	19
20	21	22	23	24	25	26
27	28	29	30			

July 2010

Sun.	Mon.	Tue.	Wed.	Thu.	Fri.	Sat.
				1	2	3
4	5	6	7	8	9	10
11	12	13	14	15	16	17
18	19	20	21	22	23	24
25	26	27	28	29	30	31

August 2010

Sun.	Mon.	Tue.	Wed.	Thu.	Fri.	Sat.
1	2	3	4	5	6	7
8	9	10	11	12	13	14
15	16	17	18	19	20	21
22	23	24	25	26	27	28
29	30	31				

September 2010

Sun.	Mon.	Tue.	Wed.	Thu.	Fri.	Sat.
			1	2	3	4
5	6	7	8	9	10	11
12	13	14	15	16	17	18
19	20	21	22	23	24	25
26	27	28	29	30		

October 2010

Sun.	Mon.	Tue.	Wed.	Thu.	Fri.	Sat.
					1	2
3	4	5	6	7	8	9
10	11	12	13	14	15	16
17	18	19	20	21	22	23
24/31	25	26	27	28	29	30

November 2010

Sun.	Mon.	Tue.	Wed.	Thu.	Fri.	Sat.
	1	2	3	4	5	6
7	8	9	10	11	12	13
14	15	16	17	18	19	20
21	22	23	24	25	26	27
28	29	30				

December 2010

Sun.	Mon.	Tue.	Wed.	Thu.	Fri.	Sat.
			1	2	3	4
5	6	7	8	9	10	11
12	13	14	15	16	17	18
19	20	21	22	23	24	25
26	27	28	29	30	31	

C MAKE IT PERSONAL. What is your favorite holiday in your country or in the U.S.? Why? What do you do on that day?

_____

_____

_____

A Complete the sentences. Use the past forms of the verbs in parentheses.

1. Diego (**go**) _____ went _____ to school in Atlanta.

2. Melissa (**not get**) _____ a job at a bank.

3. Ahmed (**come**) _____ to New York in 2007.

4. Juana (**make**) _____ good money working in a hospital.

5. Katia's parents (**grow**) _____ up in Lebanon.

6. I (**not take**) _____ any classes last year.

7. Roberto's parents (**get married**) _____ in the United States.

B Read the statements. Write negative statements.

1. Diana left home at age 18.

   _Diana didn't leave home at age 18_____. She left home at age 22.

2. Jun got a job in a cafeteria.

   _____. He got a job at a hotel.

3. I had a big wedding when I got married.

   _____. I had a small wedding.

4. Marcos went to a community college to study business.

   _____. He went to study computers.

5. Estelle began her new job yesterday.

   _____. She began last week.

6. My mother made my wedding dress.

   _____. My aunt made it.

C Unscramble the questions. Then write short answers.

1. **A:** (you / did / have / a big wedding) <u>Did you have a big wedding?</u>

   B: No, <u>   I didn't   </u>. I had a small wedding.

2. **A:** (graduate / you / last year / did) _____

   B: Yes, _____. I graduated last December.

3. **A:** (did / get / a job at a bank / Javad) _____

   B: No, _____. He got a job at a school.

4. **A:** (Lin / did / meet / in 2002 / her husband) _____

   B: Yes, _____. They met in January, 2002.

5. **A:** (a teacher / always want / did / to be / Laila?) _____

   B: No, _____. She wanted to be a nurse.

6. **A:** (a small city / did / grow up / you / in) _____

   B: No, _____. I grew up in a big city.

D Complete the conversations. Write questions. Use the correct forms of the words in parentheses.

1. **A:** (your son / born / U.S.) <u>Was your son born in the U.S.?</u>

   B: No, he wasn't. He was born in Honduras.

2. **A:** (Santos / grow up / in California) _____

   B: Yes, he did. He grew up in San Diego.

3. **A:** (your brothers / move / to the United States) _____

   B: No, they didn't. Both of my brothers live in China.

4. **A:** (you / born / in Russia) _____

   B: Yes, I was. I was born in Saint Petersburg.

5. **A:** (Magda / take / English classes last month) _____

   B: No, she didn't. She had to take care of her baby.

BEFORE YOU READ

Scan the article in Exercise B. Who is Howard Schultz? In what year did Howard

get a job at Starbucks? _____

_____

READ

Play track 20. Listen. Read the article.

Howard Schultz:
The Story of
Starbucks

★

★

★

★

Howard Schultz was born in 1953. He grew up in Brooklyn, New York. His family lived in a poor neighborhood. His father worked as a delivery driver. When Howard's father broke his leg and lost his job, the family had no health insurance. The family had a difficult time.

Howard hoped for a better life. In 1975, he graduated from Northern Michigan University. He was the first in his family to graduate from college.

In 1982, Howard got a job at a store in Seattle named Starbucks. The store sold coffee beans and educated customers about the different kinds of coffee. In 1983, Howard took a vacation in Italy. He noticed that there was a coffee shop in every neighborhood. The coffee shops were popular places for people to meet. He thought that Starbucks should serve food and drinks, too. He talked to the owners of Starbucks, but they didn't want to open a restaurant.

That didn't stop Howard. In 1985, Howard left Starbucks and started his own coffee shops. They were a big success. In 1987, Howard bought the Starbucks store and used the name for his company.

Starbucks grew quickly and is now the largest coffee shop company in the world. There are over 15,000 Starbucks coffee shops in 43 countries. Success has made Howard rich, but he didn't forget his early life. Starbucks offers full benefits, including health insurance, to both full-time and part-time employees. "I wanted to create the kind of company that my father never had a chance to work for," Howard said. In 2008, *Fortune* magazine named Starbucks the 7th best place to work in the United States.

Source: www.starbucks.com

CHECK YOUR UNDERSTANDING

A Read the article again. Then read the statements. Circle *True* or *False*.
Correct the false statements.

1. Howard's family lived in a ~~rich~~ *poor* neighborhood in New York. True **(False)**

2. Howard's family had a difficult time when his father got hurt. True False

3. Howard didn't graduate from college. True False

4. In 1982, Starbucks sold coffee drinks and sandwiches. True False

5. Howard wanted to open a coffee shop after he took a trip to Italy. True False

6. Howard bought the Starbucks store in 1987. True False

7. There are 43,000 Starbucks coffee shops in the United States. True False

8. Part-time employees can get health insurance at Starbucks. True False

B Complete the time line of Howard Schultz's life. Write the correct years or
milestones in the boxes.

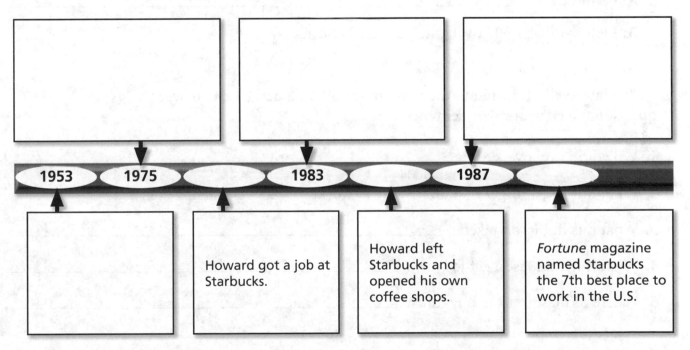

1953 — 1975 — ( ) — 1983 — ( ) — 1987 — ( )

	Howard got a job at Starbucks.	Howard left Starbucks and opened his own coffee shops.	*Fortune* magazine named Starbucks the 7th best place to work in the U.S.

A Complete the conversations. Read the replies, and then write information questions. Use the words in parentheses.

1. **A:** (**Why**) _Why did you oversleep?_____

   B: I overslept because I stayed up late last night.

2. **A:** (**When**) _____

   B: I had car trouble on Wednesday. My sister gave me a ride to work.

3. **A:** (**Where**) _____

   B: I found my wallet in my jacket pocket. I forgot to take it out.

4. **A:** (**What**) _____

   B: We went on a fishing trip last weekend. It rained the whole time!

5. **A:** (**Why**) _____

   B: I took the wrong bus because I didn't have a bus map.

6. **A:** (**What time**) _____

   B: I left work at 7:30 last night. I was really busy.

B Play track 21. Listen to the story of Jason's bad day. Then answer the questions. Write complete sentences.

1. Why did Jason oversleep? _____

2. What did Jason forget first on his way to work? _____

3. What bus did Jason take? _____

4. What time did Jason get to work? _____

5. Where did Jason try to buy lunch? _____

C Look at the pictures. The Carlson family took a trip last year. What problems did they have? Write sentences.

1. *The Carlson family got stuck in traffic.*

2. _____

3. _____

4. _____

5. _____

D MAKE IT PERSONAL. Have you ever had problems on a vacation? What happened? How did you feel?

_____

_____

Lesson 1: Vocabulary

A Match the health problems with the pictures.

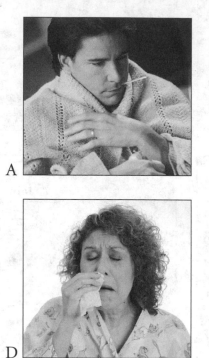
A

B

C

D

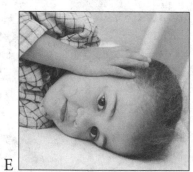
E

F

G

H

I

1. __A__ the chills

2. _____ a cold

3. _____ a cough

4. _____ an earache

5. _____ a headache

6. _____ heartburn

7. _____ a sore throat

8. _____ a stiff neck

9. _____ an upset stomach

B Complete the sentences. Underline the correct word. If the health problem has no word before it, underline *no word*.

1. Min-Ji feels hot. She has <u>a</u> / **the** fever.

2. I feel cold. I have **a** / **the** chills.

3. Huang can't eat. He has **a** / **an** upset stomach.

4. Is there a bathroom nearby? I have **the** / (**no word**) diarrhea.

5. Call a doctor now! Mr. Barrios has **the** / (**no word**) chest pains.

6. My arm is red! I have **a** / (**no word**) rash.

7. No onions, please. Onions give me **a** / (**no word**) heartburn.

8. Ms. Wilson can't turn her head. She has **a** / **the** stiff neck.

9. My brother can't talk today. He has **a** / **an** sore throat.

10. The baby sounds very sick. He has **a** / **the** cough.

C Play track 22. Listen. Complete the postcard with the health problems you hear.

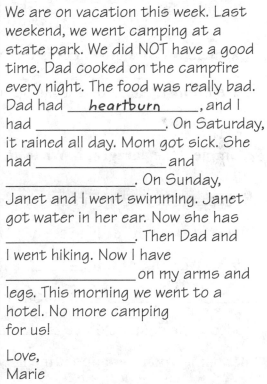

Dear Grandma,

We are on vacation this week. Last weekend, we went camping at a state park. We did NOT have a good time. Dad cooked on the campfire every night. The food was really bad. Dad had ___heartburn___, and I had _____. On Saturday, it rained all day. Mom got sick. She had _____ and _____. On Sunday, Janet and I went swimming. Janet got water in her ear. Now she has _____. Then Dad and I went hiking. Now I have _____ on my arms and legs. This morning we went to a hotel. No more camping for us!

Love,
Marie

A Complete the conversation. Underline the correct word.

Receptionist: Good morning, Dr. Quintana's office.

Carmen: Hi, this is Carmen Ruiz. I have an appointment (1) **on** / **in** Wednesday morning.

Receptionist: Yes, Mrs. Ruiz. Your appointment is (2) **at** / **in** 10:30.

Carmen: I need to change it. Can I come (3) **on** / **in** the afternoon?

Receptionist: I'm sorry. We don't take appointments (4) **in** / **on** Wednesday afternoons. Our office closes (5) **on** / **at** 1:00.

Carmen: Can I come this afternoon?

Receptionist: Well, we're closed for lunch (6) **at** / **from** 12:00 (7) **to** / **by** 1:00. But let me see here. . . . I have an opening (8) **from** / **in** an hour. Can you get here (9) **in** / **by** 11:00?

Carmen: Yes, my office is very close.

Receptionist: All right. I'll change your appointment to today, at 11:00.

B Complete the paragraph. Write *at*, *by*, *in*, *on*, or *from . . . to*.

Suzanne has a dentist appointment ___on___ January 5th at 8:00. Suzanne arrives 8:02, but
<u> </u>
1

the dentist is not ready to see her. His office is always busy. The receptionist says "Please have

a seat. We will call you _____ a few minutes." But Suzanne sits in the waiting room
                              2

_____ 8:00 _____ 8:30. She is a little worried. She starts work _____ 9:30. She needs
3   4   5

to leave the dentist's office _____ 9:15 or she will be late. Finally, the dental assistant calls
                               6

her name. After her appointment, Suzanne makes her next appointment. Her next

appointment is _____ six months. And it is _____ a Saturday morning, so she doesn't
                7   8

have to worry about being late for work!

C Read the appointment card. Then answer the questions. Write complete sentences.

```
            Downtown Health Clinic
          10 Central Street, Newtown, KS
                (313) 555-1234
         Hours: 7 A.M. – 7 P.M. Mon. – Fri.,
         7 A.M. – 5 P.M. Sat., Closed Sundays

 Michael Park    has an appointment with Dr.    Bernard

 Date: Thursday, November 19    Time:    3:45 P.M.

   New patients: Please arrive 20 minutes before appointment time.
   Please call 24 hours before appointment to change or cancel.
```

1. What day of the week is the patient's appointment?

   The appointment is on Thursday.

2. What is the date of the appointment?

   _____

3. What is the doctor's name?

   _____

4. What is the phone number of the clinic?

   _____

5. What street is the clinic on?

   _____

6. When does the clinic open on Mondays?

   _____

7. What time does the clinic close on Saturdays?

   _____

8. Imagine it is now 3:20 P.M. on November 19. How soon is the patient's
   appointment at the clinic?

   _____

9. The patient has never been to the clinic before? What time should he arrive at the clinic?

   _____

A Read the definitions. Match the definitions with the words from the box. Write the words on the lines.

> dosage   expiration date   over-the-counter (OTC) medicine
> ~~patient~~   prescription   refill
> warning

1. The person who sees a doctor for medical help: _____patient_____

2. The date you should throw away medicine: _____

3. Medicine you can buy without an order from a doctor: _____

4. An order for medicine from a doctor: _____

5. The amount of medicine you take and when you take it: _____

6. The number of times you can get more medicine: _____

7. Information about a danger: _____

B Read the medicine label. Then read the statements. Circle *True* or *False*.

1. Take this medicine for a headache.   **True**   (**False**)

2. Take 2 tablets every hour.   **True**   **False**

3. Don't take more than 2 tablets in one day.   **True**   **False**

4. Children age 12 and older can take this medicine.   **True**   **False**

5. You must not use this medicine after July 2012.   **True**   **False**

UPSET STOMACH RELIEF

Active Ingredient: Calcium Carbonate USP 1,000 mg

Uses: Relieves heartburn and upset stomach

Directions:
• Take 2 tablets every hour, as needed.

Warnings:
• Do not take more than 8 tablets in 24 hours.
• If you are taking a prescription medicine, ask your doctor before taking this product.
• Not for children under 12.
• Keep out of reach of children.

Expiration date: 01/2011

C Read the prescription medicine label. Answer the questions.

1. Who is this prescription for? _Sarah Carlton_

2. What part of the body is the medicine for? _____

3. How much medicine does Sarah take? _____

4. How often does she take the medicine? _____

5. How many refills can she get? _____

6. What is the expiration date? _____

GREENVILLE DRUGSTORE

Doctor: Alfred Finley, MD
Patient: Sarah Carlton
Dosage: Put four drops in each eye every 4 to 6 hours for four days.
Warning: For the eyes only. Do not use with children under 12.
Polymazin B
No refills
Expiration date: 3/25/2013

D Play track 23. Listen to a customer talking to a pharmacist. Complete the conversation with the words you hear.

Pharmacist: Mr. Bronson, your prescription is ready. Is this the first time you are

taking Naproxen?

Mr. Bronson: Yes, it is. How much do I take?

Pharmacist: Take _____ tablets _____ a day.

Mr. Bronson: Do I take them with _____?

Pharmacist: Yes. Take the tablets at breakfast, lunch, and dinner.

Mr. Bronson: And how long do I take them?

Pharmacist: _____.

Mr. Bronson: All right.

Pharmacist: This medicine can make you feel _____ or nauseous.

If this happens, stop taking the medicine and call your

_____.

Mr. Bronson: OK.

Pharmacist: Do you understand these _____?

Mr. Bronson: Yes, I do. Thank you.

A Complete the sentences. Use the past forms of the verbs in parentheses.

1. Oscar (**get**) _____got_____ hurt during a baseball game.

2. The new cook (**cut**) _____ her hand with a knife yesterday morning.

3. Jorge (**have**) _____ a car accident a year ago. He (**hurt**) _____

   his back.

4. Mrs. Henderson (**break**) _____ a tooth. She had to go to the dentist.

5. In-Ho (**fall**) _____ on the stairs. He (**sprain**) _____ his wrist.

B Complete the sentences. Use the past tense of the words in the box.

> fall   ~~have~~   sprain

1. Maria _____had_____ a bad accident in her house. She _____ down

   the stairs, and she _____ her arm.

> break   get   go

2. Andrew _____ hurt at work. He _____ his ankle, and he

   _____ to the emergency room.

> get   have   take

3. Mei-Lin _____ sick last week. She _____ the flu.

   I _____ her to the doctor.

C Look at the pictures. What happened? Write a sentence to describe each person's injury. Use the past tense.

1. _He hurt his back._ 4. _____

2. _____ 5. _____

3. _____ 6. _____

D MAKE IT PERSONAL. Describe a time when you or someone you know got hurt. What happened? Write sentences. Use the simple past tense.

My sister broke her arm when she was 11 years old.

She fell from a tree.

_____

_____

_____

BEFORE YOU READ

Scan the article. Look at the words in bold. What are four ways to cure a headache?

_____   _____

_____   _____

READ

Play track 24. Listen. Read the article.

HOW DO YOU CURE A HEADACHE?

Everyone gets headaches at one time or another. But people have different ways to relieve their pain. Many people take over-the-counter medicine, such as aspirin or pain reliever. But some people use home remedies. These are ways to treat an illness with food, plants, or common items around the house. People from around the world have different home remedies for headaches. Here are just a few. Try one the next time you get a headache!

➡ Hot and cold

Some home remedies use hot or cold temperatures to cure headaches. In England, some people take hot baths or showers. They let the hot water warm the backs of their necks. In Ecuador, people wet a cloth with cold water and hold it to their foreheads for fifteen minutes.

➡ Massage

Many people use massage to relieve headache pain. In Argentina, people press on the bridge of their noses, moving their fingers in small circles. In Canada, they massage a spot behind their ears. In China, they massage a spot on their hands between the thumb and pointing finger.

➡ Food

Some home remedies for headaches use food. In Japan, they eat a soup made with ginger, hot water, honey, and potato. In Morocco, people drink a tea made with mint, lime, garlic, and honey. Sometimes people don't eat the food they use; they put it on their bodies. In Lebanon, they cut potatoes into slices and place them on their foreheads.

➡ Aroma

Can smells cure a headache? Maybe! Some people in the United States heat water and apple vinegar on a stove and breathe in the strong aroma. Other people use the aroma of herbs, such as peppermint and lavender.

CHECK YOUR UNDERSTANDING

A What is the main idea of the article? Circle the letter.

 a. You can use food to cure headaches.

 b. People around the world use home remedies to cure headaches.

 c. Home remedies are better than over-the-counter medicines.

B Read the article again. Match the countries and the headache remedies.

 1. _____ Argentina

 2. _____ Ecuador

 3. _____ Morocco

 4. _____ England

 5. _____ Canada

 6. _____ Lebanon

 7. _____ United States

 8. _____ China

 9. _____ Japan

 a. massage your hands

 b. place a potato slice on your forehead

 c. drink soup with ginger, hot water, honey, and potato

 d. massage behind your ears

 e. put cold cloths on your forehead

 f. drink tea with mint, lime, garlic, and honey

 g. massage your nose

 h. put hot water on your neck

 i. breathe aromas with vinegar or herbs

C MAKE IT PERSONAL. Do you know any home remedies from your country? Do you use home remedies?

In Pakistan, we eat an apple with some salt to cure a headache. It is better than aspirin!

_____

_____

_____

A Complete the sentences. Underline *for* or *because*.

1. Hector took some cold medicine **for** / <u>**because**</u> he had the flu.

2. Cesar has bad heartburn. He went to the doctor **for** / **because** a prescription.

3. Hua had a headache. He went to the drugstore **for** / **because** some pain reliever.

4. Aunt Rita's foot is swollen **for** / **because** she fell in the bathtub. She needs to buy a rubber safety mat.

5. Mrs. Hwang needs new glasses. She called her eye doctor **for** / **because** an appointment.

6. I need to call my boss. I can't go to work today **for** / **because** I hurt my ankle.

B Complete the sentences. Write *because* or *for*.

1. My daughter Ju-Yeon didn't go to school today _____because_____ she didn't feel well.

   I went to the drugstore _____ some flu medicine.

2. Eva took her baby to the clinic _____ she needed a checkup. The doctor

   asked her to come back next week _____ a blood test.

3. I went the dental clinic _____ I had a bad toothache. I had to wait a long

   time _____ they were very busy.

4. I went to the doctor _____ a flu shot. I wanted to get the shot

   _____ I had the flu last year and I missed a lot of work.

5. Camila always misses class. Last week she was absent _____ she had a sore

   throat. Today she's absent _____ she has to work.

C Look at the pictures. Answer the questions. Write complete sentences. Use the words in parentheses. There may be more than one correct answer.

1. Why did Roberto go to the drugstore?

   (because) <u>He went to the drugstore because</u>

   <u>he needed eye drops.</u>

   (for) _____

   _____

2. Why did Sharon miss work?

   (because) _____

   _____

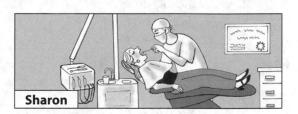

3. Why did Haseem call 911?

   (because) _____

   _____

4. Why did Isabel go to the doctor?

   (because) _____

   _____

   (for) _____

   _____

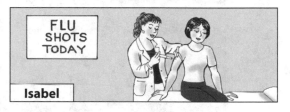

5. Why did Anton call his supervisor?

   (because) _____

   _____

Lesson 1: Vocabulary

A Match the words to form a job duty. Write the letter on the line.

1. _d_ prepare   a. computer hardware

2. ____ stock   b. shelves

3. ____ install   c. materials

4. ____ unload   d. food

5. ____ record   e. patient information

6. ____ supervise   f. employees

B Look at the pictures. Write the job duty on the line. Use job duties from Exercise A.

1. _prepare food_

2. _____

3. _____

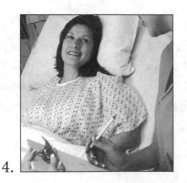

4. _____

5. _____

6. _____

C Look at the pictures. Write the job title and two job duties for each picture. There may be more than one correct answer.

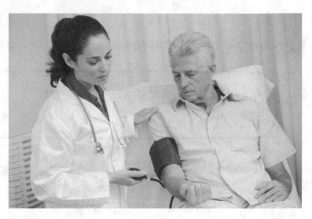

1. Job title: *food service worker*

   Job duties: *prepare food, clean kitchen equipment*

2. Job title: ―――――――――――

   Job duties: ―――――――――――

3. Job title: ――――――――――――――

   Job duties: ――――――――――――――

4. Job title: ――――――――――

   Job duties: ――――――――――

D MAKE IT PERSONAL. Think of three people you know. Write their job titles and list their job duties.

Blanca—stock clerk. stock shelves, assist customers

―――――――――――――――――――――――――――

―――――――――――――――――――――――――――

―――――――――――――――――――――――――――

A Complete the sentences. Use *can* or *can't* and a verb from the box.

> lift   operate   order   speak
>
> prepare   ~~type~~   use

1. Nadya uses a computer a lot. She ____can type____ about 44 words per minute.

2. Lola doesn't know how to drive. She _____ a forklift.

3. Thanh only speaks Vietnamese and English. He _____ Spanish.

4. Delma doesn't know how to use a computer. She _____ a word-processing program.

5. Sahar is a cook at a restaurant. She _____ food.

6. Chen knows what we need for the office. He _____ supplies.

7. Bao isn't very strong. He _____ boxes over 35 pounds.

B Complete the conversations. Read the answers. Write *Yes / No* questions with *can*.

1. **A:** _Can you lift heavy boxes?_

   B: No, I can't. I can't lift heavy boxes. I hurt my back.

2. **A:** _____

   B: Yes, she can. Ms. Navarro can speak English well.

3. **A:** _____

   B: Yes, he can. Diego can order more spaghetti for the kitchen.

4. **A:** _____

   B: No, I can't. I don't know how to type. But I can learn.

5. **A:** _____

   B: No, he can't. David can't work on Sundays.

C Imagine you are the manager of a supermarket. You need a new stock clerk, cashier, and food service worker. You need to interview job applicants for each position. Write three questions you can ask the applicants.

stock clerk

Can you lift heavy boxes?

_____

_____

cashier

_____

_____

_____

food service worker

_____

_____

_____

D Look at the applicants and their skills. Choose one person for each supermarket job in Exercise C. Explain your choices.

Applicants	Skills						
	use a cash register	lift heavy boxes	stock shelves	operate a forklift	order supplies	prepare food	clean kitchen equip-ment
Ignacio		✓	✓	✓	✓		
Marie	✓	✓	✓			✓	✓
Chan			✓		✓	✓	✓

I'm going to give Ignacio the stock clerk job because...

_____

_____

_____

Ⓐ Read the help-wanted ads. Rewrite the ads using the full word for each abbreviation.

1.
> PT cashier pos. available.
> M–F, eve. Exp. req.

Part-time cashier position available. Monday–Friday, evenings. Experience required.

2.
> FT bus drivers needed.
> Mornings/afternoons,
> 11.50/hr, bnfts., driver's
> license req. Tel. (312) 555-1234

3.
> Stock clerk pos. available,
> FT, M–F/some weekends.
> No exp. req. Apply in
> person. Bring ref.

4.
> Nurse assistants wanted.
> FT, flexible hrs. Excel. bnfts.
> 2 yr. exp. req. E-mail résumé
> to jobs@allnurses.com.
> Incl. ref.

Ⓑ Read the help-wanted ads. Rewrite the ads using abbreviations. Make them as short as possible.

1.
> Part-time receptionist position available at a busy car
> sales office. Saturday–Sunday 8:00–4:00. The job
> includes handling phone calls and greeting customers.
> No experience required. We will train the right person.
> Telephone Gary's Classic Cars (312) 555-1234.

2.
> Full-time warehouse assistant wanted in large company.
> Monday–Friday 7:00–4:00. Must be able to lift up to
> 50 lbs. Experience required in operating a forklift. We
> offer excellent pay, including benefits and vacation.

C Read the help-wanted ads. Then read the statements. Circle *True* or *False*.

HELP WANTED		
Office Assistant FT office assistant pos. available. Excel. computer skills req., 3 yrs. office exp. pref. Bnfts. incl. health insurance and vacation. E-mail resume to hr@modelagency.com. No calls please.	**Night Shift Manager** FT. pos. available in paper warehouse. Night shift (10 pm–7 am.) Full bnfts. and vacation after 3 months. 4 yrs. exp. supervising employees req. Apply in person only M–F 1 pm–5 pm. 325 Lincoln Street. Bring ref.	**Gardener** FT summer help wanted at Luis Landscaping. 05/01–10/01. M–F 7:30 am–3:00 pm. $15.75/hr. No exp. req. Tel. 321 555-1234. Ask for Luis.

1. The office assistant job is part time.   **True** (**False**)

2. You need computer skills for the office assistant job.   **True**   **False**

3. You call the company to apply for the office assistant job.   **True**   **False**

4. The night manager shift is from 1:00 P.M. to 5:00 P.M.   **True**   **False**

5. You get benefits after three months at the night manager job.   **True**   **False**

6. You go to 325 Lincoln Street to apply for the manager job.   **True**   **False**

7. The gardener job is from May to October only.   **True**   **False**

8. You need experience for the gardener job.   **True**   **False**

D Read about Gilbert Reyes. Then look at the help-wanted ads in Exercise C. Which job is the best match for Gilbert? Explain your answer.

> Gilbert Reyes is looking for a job. In Puerto Rico, he was the assistant manager in an office for four years. He needs to work full time. He likes working in an office. He needs a job with health benefits because he has a wife and a six-year-old son. Gilbert can supervise employees, use a computer, and type. He has good references from his old job in Puerto Rico.

_____

_____

_____

A Complete the sentences. Write *ago, in,* or *later.*

David Ho was born in Taiwan ___in___ 1952. His father went to the

United States to work. Nine years _____, Mr. Ho brought his wife

2

and two sons to the U.S. David was twelve years old. The family lived

in Los Angeles. David went to school, but he didn't understand

English. He studied very hard. He learned English _____ six

3

months. David went to college and studied medicine. He became a

doctor. _____ the 1990s, he studied a terrible new disease called

4

AIDS. Dr. Ho made medicine for people who had AIDS.

_____ 1996, Dr. Ho received Time Magazine's "Man of the Year" award. Now people with

5

AIDS can live longer than they did ten years _____.

6

B 🔘 Play track 25. Listen to stories about two immigrants to the U.S.
Complete the time lines. Write the dates and milestones.

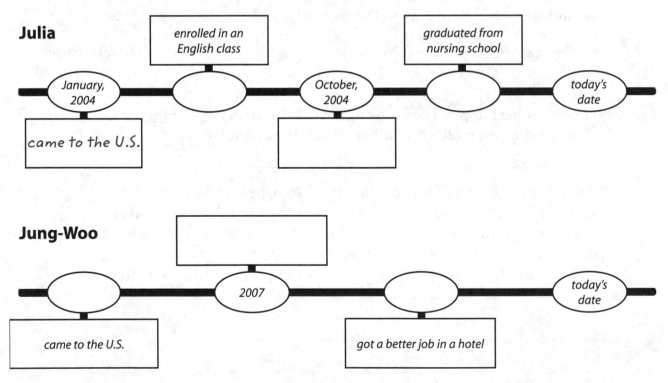

C Look at the time line. Complete the paragraph about Arnold Schwarzenegger's life. Use *ago, in,* and *later*.

ARNOLD SCHWARZENEGGER

	wins Mr. Universe bodybuilding title		stars in first movie: *Hercules in New York*		becomes a U.S. citizen		becomes governor of California
1947	1967	1968	1970	1982	1983	1986	2003
born in Austria		moves to the U.S.	stars in the hit movie *The Terminator*			marries TV news star Maria Shriver	

Arnold Schwarzenegger was born in 1947 in Austria. _____

_____

_____

_____

D MAKE IT PERSONAL. Complete the sentences about your own life. Use true information.

1. _____ last week.

2. _____ three months ago.

3. _____ in 2007.

BEFORE YOU READ

Look at the title of the article and the photo. Predict: What is the topic of the article?

_____

READ

🔘 **Play track 26. Listen. Read the article. Was your guess in Before You Read correct?**

HOME	JOB LISTINGS	POST RESUME	CAREER ADVICE	HELP

Job Interview Tips ◀

You're looking for a job. You complete an application, and then you get a phone call to come in for an interview. You are happy and excited, but then you begin to worry. What do you do now? How can you prepare for the interview? Remember that an interview is a chance for the hiring manager to learn if you are a good match for the job. It is also a chance for you to learn about the job and decide if you really want it. There are many things you can do to make the interview a success. Here are some tips.

- Wear the right clothes for the job. Look neat and clean. Don't wear a lot of jewelry, makeup, or perfume. Don't chew gum, eat, or drink during the interview.
- Arrive fifteen minutes early. You can use the time to use the restroom, comb your hair, relax, or fill out paperwork.
- Act confident. Yes, you are nervous, but stay calm. Smile, make eye contact, stand or sit straight, and give a firm handshake.
- Be ready to talk about your work history and your job skills. Explain why you think you are a good match for the job.
- Be formal but friendly. The interview may be casual and relaxed, but don't make jokes or use informal language or slang. Don't talk about age, religion, or politics.
- Be prepared for the question, "Why did you leave your last job?" If you were fired from a job, be honest about what happened. Stay positive and explain what you learned from the experience.

CHECK YOUR UNDERSTANDING

A Read the article again. What is the purpose of the article?

a. to help people do well in a job interview

b. to explain how to complete a job application

c. to show how to answer common interview questions

B Read about Dominique's job interview. Did Dominique follow the advice in the article? What did she do correctly? What mistakes did she make? Write sentences.

> Dominique had a job interview at a hotel. She wanted to look nice. She ironed her shirt and pants. She wore a little more jewelry and perfume than usual. The interview was at 9:00. Dominique arrived at the hotel at 8:58. She had to hurry. She arrived at the manager's office at exactly 9:00. She met the manager and gave him a firm handshake. They talked about Dominique's work history and skills. Dominique was nervous, but she smiled and made eye contact. The manager asked Dominique why she left her last job. Dominique explained that she was fired. She talked about why she didn't like her last boss. The manager thanked Dominique. He said, "I'll let you know about the job next week."

Dominique wore too much jewelry. _____

_____

_____

_____

C MAKE IT PERSONAL. Think about a job interview you or someone you know had. Answer the questions.

1. Did you follow the tips in the article? _____

2. Did you make any mistakes? _____

3. What other job interview tips can you give? _____

A Complete the conversations. Write *and* or *or*.

1. **A:** What's your availability?

   B: I can work weekdays __and__ weekends. I need all the hours you can give me.

2. **A:** Can you work Monday through Friday?

   B: No, I can't work on Tuesdays _____ Thursdays. I have classes on those days.

3. **A:** Does your class meet twice a week?

   B: Yes, it meets on Monday _____ Wednesday mornings.

4. **A:** Do you have transportation to work?

   B: Yes, I do. I can take the bus _____ get a ride from my husband.

5. **A:** Do you prefer first shift _____ second shift?

   B: I prefer first shift. I have an English class at night. But I'm flexible.

B Play track 27. Listen to the job applicants talk about their availability. Complete the job applications. Check the boxes.

1.
When can you work? Check the boxes.
❏ Saturday ❏ Sunday

2.
When can you work? Check the boxes.
❏ first shift ❏ second shift

3.
When can you work? Check the boxes.
❏ breakfast shift ❏ lunch shift
❏ dinner shift

4.
When can you work? Check the boxes.
❏ weekdays ❏ weekends
❏ days ❏ evenings

C Imagine you are a manager at a shoe store. Read your employees' availability. Then complete the schedule. Choose one employee for each shift. Each employee must work twenty hours.

Rosa

I can work mornings or afternoons. I can't work on Wednesday or Friday mornings because I have a class. I can't work on weekends.

Fang

I can't work on Fridays or Saturday mornings. I prefer to work the afternoon shift.

Paul

I can't work on Tuesdays or Thursdays. I can work on weekends. I prefer to work mornings.

Coffee Stop Cafe	Employee Schedule		April 7 – April 12			
	Mon.	Tue.	Wed.	Thu.	Fri.	Sat.
Morning Shift 6:30–11:30 A.M.						
Afternoon Shift 11:00 A.M.–4:00 P.M.						

D MAKE IT PERSONAL. Imagine you are looking for a job. Complete the job application about your own work availability.

When can you work? Check the boxes.

❏ Mon. ❏ Tues. ❏ Wed. ❏ Thurs. ❏ Fri. ❏ Sat. ❏ Sun.

❏ mornings ❏ afternoons ❏ evenings

Lesson 1: Vocabulary

A Look at the pictures. Write the school subjects. Use the words from the box.

> art   community service   language arts/English   math
> music   ~~P.E. (physical education)~~   science   social studies/history
> technology

1. _P.E. (physical education)_

2. _____

3. _____

4. _____

5. _____

6. _____

7. _____

8. _____

9. _____

B Read what the students say about their favorite school subjects. Complete each statement with a school subject from Exercise A.

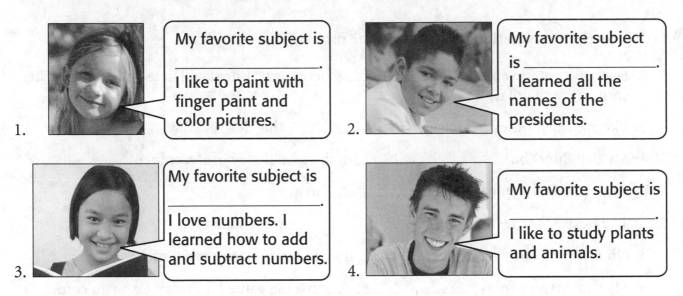

1. My favorite subject is _____. I like to paint with finger paint and color pictures.

2. My favorite subject is _____. I learned all the names of the presidents.

3. My favorite subject is _____. I love numbers. I learned how to add and subtract numbers.

4. My favorite subject is _____. I like to study plants and animals.

C Read the descriptions of classes in the high school course catalog. Write the title of each course with a school subject from Exercise A.

Greenville High School
Grade 9 Course List

1. Course: _music_____

   Students will learn how to read music and play one of these instruments: piano, drums, violin, or clarinet.

2. Course: _____

   Students will learn how to play team sports (soccer, volleyball) and individual sports (swimming, running).

3. Course: _____

   Students will work thirty hours with an organization that helps people. Students will help at a food bank, teach younger children, or clean around lakes and rivers.

4. Course: _____

   Students will read and write stories, learn grammar, and discuss literature.

5. Course: _____

   Students will learn basic computer skills, such as using the Internet and using word processing programs.

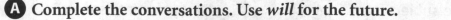

A Complete the conversations. Use *will* for the future.

1. **A:** Esteban (**not have**) _____won't have_____ school next Thursday. There's a parent-teacher conference that day.

   B: I know. My mother (**watch**) _____ the kids that day.

2. **A:** My daughter (**be**) _____ in the school play in December.

   B: How exciting! I (**plan**) _____ to go.

3. **A:** The next PTO meeting (**be**) _____ on January 17.

   B: Oh no! I (**not be**) _____ there. I have to babysit my niece.

4. **A:** My soccer team (**play**) _____ in a big game on Friday. Can you come?

   B: Well, I have to work that night, but I (**try**) _____ to change my schedule.

B Complete the letter. Use *will* for future and the words in the box. Use contractions if possible.

> | | | | | |
> |---|---|---|---|---|
> | be | give | go | ~~have~~ | play |
> | present | show | sing | visit | |

Hi Mom,

Next Tuesday morning, Jiao's school ___will have___ a special event—Grandparents' Day. The children are
                                      1

planning a lot of fun activities. The grandparents _____ the children's classrooms in the morning.
                                                          2

Each class _____ a special program for the grandparents. Children in music classes _____
                3   **4**

and dance. Children and their grandparents _____ computer games in the technology classes. The
                                                 5

art classes _____ the grandparents the pictures they made. At noon, everyone _____ to
                 6   **7**

the cafeteria for a special lunch. The principal _____ the grandparents books they can read with their
                                                       8

grandchildren. I think it _____ a really nice event. I hope you can come!
                               9

Love, Luli

C  **Play track 28. Listen to a high school announcement. Complete the sentences with the words you hear.**

Good morning, students. We have a busy week at Greenville Middle School. The Music Club _____ a bake sale today. Club members _____ cookies and other baked goods from 11:30 to 12:30 in the cafeteria. The Technology Club _____ in the library today at 4:00. Bad news, Greenville basketball fans. There _____ a basketball game on Wednesday. The Greenville Tigers _____ their next home game on Monday at 7:00 P.M. Don't forget there _____ a Back-to-school Night for parents on Thursday at 7:30. Your parents _____ your classes and meet your teachers . . . but they _____ your homework for you! And finally, on Friday, the seventh grade class _____ a field trip to the Greenville Science Museum. Please remember to bring a bag lunch. Thank you and have a good day.

D **Read the school event notice. What will the students do on Community Service Day? Write sentences using *will*.**

Greenville High School

Community Service Day

Greenville High School will have a Community Service Day on Friday, May 18th, from 8:00 A.M. to 12:00 P.M. This is a chance for students to help others and to show they care about their community. Students will participate in the following projects:

- 9th Grade: collect cans of food for "Food for All" organization
- 10th Grade: read stories to children at the Greenville Children's Hospital
- 11th Grade: paint benches and playground equipment at Silver Beach
- 12th Grade: clean up garbage and plant flowers at Greenville Park

_____

_____

_____

_____

A Complete the conversations. Choose the correct response. Circle the letter.

1. **A:** Oak Grove Middle School.

   B: _____

   (a.) Hello. May I speak to Mrs. Dawson, please?   b. Please call back.

2. **A:** May I speak to Ms. Wilson, please?

   B: _____

   a. OK. I'll give her the message.   b. I'm sorry. She's not in the office
                                                        right now.

3. **A:** I'm sorry. Mr. Green is not available right now. Can I take a message?

   B: _____

   a. Please ask him to call me back.   b. I'll give him the message.

4. **A:** May I take a message?

   B: _____

   a. No, thank you. I'll call back later.   b. I'm sorry. He's not in the office.

5. **A:** What's your number?

   B: _____

   a. Ask Mr. Lee to call my cell phone.   b. It's 718-555-3456.

B Play track 29. Listen. Choose the correct response. Circle the letter.

1. a. Hello. This is Tom Smith.   b. 555-8765.

2. a. I'll ask him to call you back.   b. I'm sorry. He's not available right now.

3. a. Yes. Please ask Claudia to call me back.   b. OK. I'll give her the message.

4. a. He's not here right now.   b. All right. I'll give him your message.

5. a. Yes, thank you.   b. (404)555-8382.

C 📀 **Play track 30. Listen to the conversation. Circle the number of the correct message.**

1.
Date __10/9__ Time __11:30__

To __Mrs. Clemens__

While You Were Out

From __Mr. Roberto Santiago__

Phone __(781) 555-5454__

Message: __Please call.__
_____

2.
Date __10/9__ Time __11:30__

To __Mrs. Clemens__

While You Were Out

From __Mr. Roberto Santiago__

Phone __(718) 555-4343__

Message: __Please call.__
_____

3.
Date __10/9__ Time __11:30__

To __Mr. Roberto Santiago__

While You Were Out

From __Mrs. Clemens__

Phone __(718) 555-4343__

Message: __Will call back.__
_____

D 📀 **Play track 31. Listen to the conversation. Complete the phone message with the information you hear. Write the current date and time.**

Date _____ Time _____

To _____

While You Were Out

From _____

Phone _____

Message: _____
_____

A Complete the sentences. Underline the correct word.

1. Maya is a **good** / **well** writer. Her book report was excellent.

2. Gregory didn't pass his math test because he didn't work **careful** / **carefully**.

3. Quan got a 97 on his math exam. He studied **hard** / **hardly**.

4. It is difficult to read Pablo's papers. He doesn't write **neat** / **neatly**.

5. Anita finished her homework in half an hour. She worked **quick** / **quickly**.

6. My daughter is having trouble in science. She is a **poor** / **poorly** student in that subject.

7. The children didn't talk in the classroom. They were **quiet** / **quietly**.

B Complete the report card. Change the adjectives in the box to adverbs.
Write the adverbs on the lines.

careful	careless	clear	creative	good
hard	~~neat~~	poor	quick	quiet

Redwood Middle School

Student: Tariq Hassan
Semester: Fall

Subject	Grade	Comments
Language Arts	B	Tariq writes _____neatly_____. His handwriting is always easy to read. He makes a lot of spelling mistakes. He needs to check his spelling _____.
Math	B	Tariq learns _____. He is always the first to solve math problems on the board. Sometimes he works _____. He needs to check his answers for mistakes.
Science	C	Tariq often speaks very _____. It is difficult for other students to hear him. He needs to speak _____ and share his ideas with the class.
Music	D	Tariq does _____ on tests. He got a 65 on his final exam. He needs to study _____ next semester.
Art	A	Tariq thinks _____. He has a great imagination and a lot of new ideas. He follows directions _____. I never have to tell him something twice.

C Complete the conversations. Write the correct object pronoun.

1. **A:** Can you help Lucy with her math problems?

   B: No problem. I'll help _____.

2. **A:** Mom, I need to go to the library.

   B: OK. I'm busy tonight, but Grandma will take _____.

3. **A:** Emilio, your art project is really good!

   B: Thanks. I worked hard on _____.

4. **A:** I can't remember my spelling words.

   B: All right. Let's review _____ one more time.

5. **A:** Did my teachers talk about _____ at the parent-teacher conference?

   B: Yes, and they had good things to say!

D Complete the letter. Write the correct object pronoun.

Dear Mom,

Well, the kids got their report cards from school today. Becky and Mike both did well. I am proud of ___them___.
$\quad\quad\quad\quad$ **1**

Do you remember last semester? Becky didn't like math. She had trouble with _____.
$\quad\quad\quad\quad$ **2**
But Becky's teacher, Mr. Migdol, was very helpful. Dan and I talked to _____ after
$\quad\quad\quad\quad$ **3**
school. He told _____ about a new program called Homework Help. Now Becky meets
$\quad\quad\quad\quad$ **4**
with a student from the high school after class. The student helps _____ with
$\quad\quad\quad\quad$ **5**
homework. This semester, Becky got an A in math! And now she loves _____!
$\quad\quad\quad\quad$ **6**

Mike also did better this semester. Last semester he got a C in language arts. He did
poorly on his writing assignments. This semester he spent more time on _____. He
$\quad\quad\quad\quad$ **7**
got a B+! And Mike made a wonderful science fair project. He really worked hard on
_____. He won second prize!
8

We are looking forward to your visit next month. We miss _____!
$\quad\quad\quad\quad$ **9**
Love, Karen

BEFORE YOU READ

Look at the picture in the article. What is the girl doing?

_____

READ

Play track 32. Listen. Read the article.

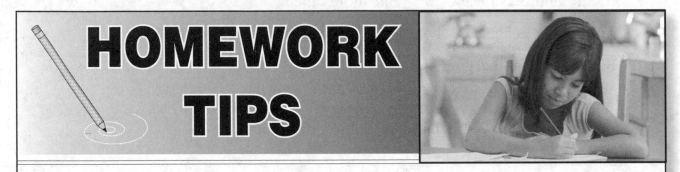

HOMEWORK TIPS

Studies show that children do better in school when their parents are involved in their schoolwork. What parents do at home is very important to a student's success. In fact, it's more important than whether a family is rich or poor, or whether parents have had a lot of education or not.

Homework helps students practice what they have learned. It gets them ready for the next day's classes. It helps students develop good work habits and attitudes. Homework also gives parents a chance to be involved in their child's education. However, getting your child to turn off the TV and do his or her homework can be difficult. Here are a few tips to improve your child's homework habits.

1. Make a homework schedule. Set a period of time for homework every day. Choose a time when your child works best. Avoid times when your child may be tired, such as just before bed.

2. Create a study area. Choose a quiet area of your home with good lighting, away from the TV. It could be a desk in the child's bedroom or a corner of the kitchen table.

3. Organize school supplies. Your child will need supplies such as pencils, pens, erasers, paper, and a dictionary. Keep these things together in one place.

4. Check homework. Keep a list of your child's homework assignments on the refrigerator. Write the date your child has to complete each assignment. Check off each assignment when your child finishes it.

5. Show you are interested. Ask about your child's day at school. Talk about the schoolwork that your child brings home. Encourage your child to read aloud a poem he or she wrote or talk about the results of a science experiment. Attend school events, such as PTO meetings, sports events, and band concerts. Tell your child how proud you are!

CHECK YOUR UNDERSTANDING

(A) **What is the purpose of the article? Circle the letter.**

a. to give homework advice to students

b. to suggest ways parents can help their children with homework

c. to stop children from watching too much TV

(B) **Look at the picture. Is the family following the advice in the article? Write about the good and bad homework habits you see in the picture.**

The son should study away from the TV. _____

_____

_____

(C) **MAKE IT PERSONAL. Do you think the tips in the article are useful? Can you add two more homework tips for parents?**

1. _____   2. _____

A Complete the sentences. Write the possessive forms of the nouns in parentheses.

1. My (**daughter**) _daughter's_ teachers are worried about her behavior. She is disrespectful and doesn't pay attention in class.

2. The (**children**) _____ art projects were all very good. The teacher displayed them in the hallway.

3. Greenville Middle school got money for computers. Now (**Ms. Wilson**) _____ room has computers for every student.

4. My (**son**) _____ science grade went from a C to a B. I think he's studying more.

5. The parent-teacher conference was a success. The (**parents**) _____ attendance was about 90 percent.

6. At the orientation, the principal reviewed the (**school**) _____ policies about clothes, attendance, and behavior.

7. My (**nephew**) _____ report card was excellent. He got an A in every subject.

B Add the missing apostrophe to each sentence.

1. Sandra went to her sons' basketball game. The two boys are both on the same team.

2. I'm worried about Marys grades. She got a bad report card this semester.

3. Melissa is a football fan. She knows all the football players names.

4. Jimmy looked at another students paper during the test. His teacher took his paper away and gave him an F.

5. Javier was fooling around in class. The teacher sent him to the principals office.

6. Mr. Murray called Bills parents. He wanted to find out why he wasn't in school.

C Read the article. Complete the sentences. Underline the correct word.

School Uniforms Debate

Should **<u>students</u> / students'** wear uniforms in school? Students, parents, and teachers have different opinions.

Many parents and teachers like the idea. Parents think uniforms are cheaper than regular **children's / childrens'** clothes. They also think it's easier to get their **kids / kid's** ready for school in the morning. "When I shop for my **kids' / kids** clothes, I don't have to buy expensive designer brands. And my **daughter's / daughters** don't waste so much time in the morning planning what they are going to wear," says Ann Carter, a Greenville mom.

Teachers say that uniforms improve **students' / students** behavior in class. "Wearing a uniform reminds **students / students'** that they are in school to learn and that they have to follow the **school's / schools'** rules," says Ted Cezus, a science teacher at Greenville Middle School.

However, most students don't like to wear uniforms. They feel that clothing is a way for people to express their personalities. "I don't want to dress the same as all of my **classmates / classmates'**, explains Tina Lynch, a student at Greenville High School. "I want to wear clothes that show who I am." **Students / Students'** disagree that a **person's / persons'** clothing changes their behavior. "You don't act better because of what you're wearing. You're still the same person inside," says Tina.

D MAKE IT PERSONAL. Did you wear a uniform when you were in school? Do you think students should wear uniforms? Explain why or why not.

_____

_____

_____

Lesson 1: Vocabulary

A Look at the pictures. Write the food container or quantity on the line. Use the words in the box.

> bag   ~~box~~   bunch   can   gallon   half-gallon

1. _____box_____   2. _____   3. _____

4. _____   5. _____   6. _____

B Which food matches each container? Complete the phrase. Circle the letter.

1. a bag of _____

   a. milk   b. eggs   ©. rice

2. a bunch of _____

   a. grapes   b. cereal   c. pickles

3. a head of _____

   a. cabbage   b. carrots   c. ice cream

4. a dozen _____

   a. donuts   b. cheese   c. orange juice

5. a box of _____

   a. water   b. cookies   c. tuna fish

6. a gallon of _____

   a. milk   b. tomatoes   c. cereal

C Match the pictures and the foods. Write the letter on the line.

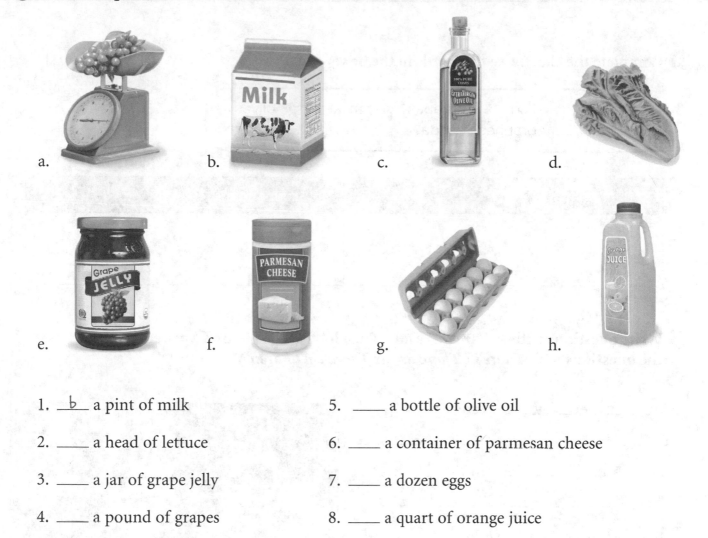

a.

b.

c.

d.

e.

f.

g.

h.

1. __b__ a pint of milk

2. ____ a head of lettuce

3. ____ a jar of grape jelly

4. ____ a pound of grapes

5. ____ a bottle of olive oil

6. ____ a container of parmesan cheese

7. ____ a dozen eggs

8. ____ a quart of orange juice

**D MAKE IT PERSONAL. What do you buy at the supermarket every week?
Make a list of items you always buy, sometimes buy, and never buy.**

I always buy…	I sometimes buy…	I never buy…
a quart of orange juice		

A **Complete the chart. Use the words in the box.**

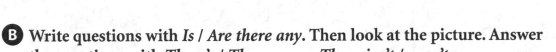

| apples | fish | grapes | milk | olives |
| onions | oranges | soda | sugar | yogurt |

Count nouns	Non-count nouns
apples	fish

B **Write questions with *Is / Are there any*. Then look at the picture. Answer the questions with *There's / There are* or *There isn't / aren't*.**

1. **A:** _____Is there any_____ bread?

   B: ____Yes, there's some on the counter.____

2. **A:** _____ fish?

   B: _____

3. **A:** _____ apples?

   B: _____

4. **A:** _____ carrots?

   B: _____

5. **A:** _____ yogurt?

   B: _____

6. **A:** _____ bananas?

   B: _____

7. **A:** _____ cheese?

   B: _____

8. **A:** _____ cereal?

   B: _____

C Complete the conversations with *How much* or *How many*.

1. **A:** _____How many_____ carrots do we need?

   B: We don't need any. I bought two bunches of carrots yesterday.

2. **A:** _____ boxes of crackers do we need for the party?

   B: Two boxes is enough.

3. **A:** _____ orange juice should I buy?

   B: None. I think there's a quart in the refrigerator.

4. **A:** _____ lettuce do you need for the salad?

   B: I have one head. I need one more.

5. **A:** _____ jars of jelly did you buy?

   B: I bought three big jars. They were on sale.

D 🎧 Play track 33. Listen. Complete the conversation. Write the words you hear. Then complete the shopping list. Write the foods Paulo needs to buy.

Paulo: I'm going to the supermarket. Do we need anything for dinner?

Clara: Well. I think I'm going to make some soup. Could

you get some _____?

Paulo: Sure. _____ do you need?

Clara: Let me check the recipe. I need _____.

Paulo: OK. _____?

Clara: Let's see. _____ carrots?

Paulo: Yes, there's _____ carrots in the

refrigerator.

Clara: That's enough. _____ olive oil?

Paulo: Yes, there's _____ olive oil in the cabinet.

Clara: Good. _____ potatoes?

Paulo: Um. No, there aren't any. I'll get _____.

Shopping List

A Match the nutrients and the definitions.

1. __c__ carbohydrates   a. It is also called *salt*.

2. ____ cholesterol   b. It helps your stomach digest food. It comes from plants.

3. ____ fiber   c. It gives you energy for several hours.

4. ____ protein   d. It gives you quick energy. Too much is not good for you.

5. ____ sodium   e. It makes your body strong.

6. ____ sugar   f. It is only in animal fat. Too much is not good for you.

B Which food does not belong in each nutrient category? Circle the letter.

1. Fiber

a.    b.   c.    d.

2. Protein

a.   b.   c.   d.

3. Carbohydrates

a.    b.   c.   d.

C Read the nutrition and ingredient labels for two cereal brands. Answer the questions.

Toasted Oats
brand cereal

Nutrition Facts
Serving Size 1 Cup (28g)
Servings Per Container 14

Amount Per Serving

Calories 100 Calories from Fat 15

Total Fat 2g

Cholesterol 0mg

Sodium 190mg

Total Carbohydrate 20g

Dietary Fiber 3g

Sugars 1g

Protein 3g

INGREDIENTS: WHOLE GRAIN OATS, CORN STARCH, SUGAR, OAT BRAN, SALT.

Fruit Rings
brand cereal

Nutrition Facts
Serving Size 1 Cup (28g)
Servings Per Container 14

Amount Per Serving

Calories 120 Calories from Fat 10

Total Fat 1g

Cholesterol 0mg

Sodium 135mg

Total Carbohydrate 25g

Dietary Fiber 1g

Sugars 16g

Protein 1g

INGREDIENTS: SUGAR, CORN FLOUR, WHEAT FLOUR, OAT FLOUR, PARTIALLY HYDROGENATED VEGETABLE OIL, SALT, CORN SYRUP, NATURAL AND ARTIFICIAL FLAVOR.

1. What is the main ingredient in Toasted Oats cereal? _whole grain oats_____

2. How much sodium is in one serving of Toasted Oats cereal? _____

3. How much protein is in one serving of Toasted Oats cereal? _____

4. How much fiber is in one serving of Toasted Oats cereal? _____

5. How much sugar is in one serving of Fruit Rings cereal? _____

6. How many carbohydrates are in one serving of Fruit Rings cereal? _____

7. How much cholesterol is in one serving of Fruit Rings cereal? _____

8. How many calories from fat are in one serving of Fruit Rings cereal? _____

D Compare the two cereal brands in Exercise C. Which cereal is better for your health? Why?

_____

_____

A Complete the conversations. Write the comparative forms of the adjectives in parentheses. Add *than*.

1. **A:** You're buying frozen pizzas?

   B: Sure. I like them. And they're (**cheap**) ___cheaper than___ pizzas from a restaurant.

2. **A:** Want some ice cream?

   B: No, I'm going to have a yogurt. It's (**healthy**) _____ ice cream.

3. **A:** Do you want fresh corn or canned corn?

   B: Fresh corn. Canned vegetables are (**salty**) _____ fresh vegetables.

4. **A:** Should I get beef or fish?

   B: Beef is (**expensive**) _____ and (**fattening**) _____ fish.

   A: OK, let's get fish.

5. **A:** Did you have the chocolate cake or the carrot cake?

   B: I had both. Go for the chocolate. It's (**delicious**) _____ the carrot cake.

B ⊙ Play track 34. Listen to the conversations. Answer the questions. Use a comparative adjective.

Conversation 1

1. Why does Angel like canned soup? _____

2. Why does Claudia prefer homemade soup? _____

Conversation 2

3. Why does Sam want to eat pizza at The Italian Café? _____

4. Why does Anne prefer frozen pizza? _____

Conversation 3

5. Why does Sally want to barbecue chicken? _____

6. Why does Evan prefer to make sandwiches? _____

C Imagine you are shopping for food. Look at the supermarket ads. Which foods will you buy? Explain your answer. Use a comparative adjective.

I'll buy frozen peas. They're more convenient than fresh peas.

1. _____
   _____
   _____

Fresh Green Peas
This week
$1.99 / pound

Frozen Green Peas
Birds Eye
Garden Peas
10 oz. bag
Only
$1.29

2. _____
   _____
   _____

Canned Pears
PEARS
CHOICE QUALITY
This week
2 cans for
$2

Fresh California Pears
On Sale
$1.49 / pound

3. _____
   _____
   _____

Orange Juice
ORANGE JUICE
Half-gallon carton
$3
Save $.50

Florida Oranges
$.99 / pound

4. _____
   _____
   _____

Fresh Salmon Steak
$6.99 / pound

Rib-Eye Steak
Special
$9.99 / pound

D MAKE IT PERSONAL. What information can you find in a supermarket ad? Do you read supermarket ads when you shop for food?

_____

_____

READ

Play track 35. Listen. Read the article.

How Do You Save Money on Food?

The cost of food is going up. Your grocery bill seems to get higher every time you visit the supermarket. The trouble is, you have to eat. So how can you fill your stomach without emptying your wallet? We talked to shoppers from around the U.S. about how they save money at the supermarket. Here are some of their ideas.

"My family calls me Coupon Mom. I look for coupons in the mail and cut them out of the Sunday newspaper. I usually go shopping with about 20 coupons, and I save between $10–$15. If the store gives **double coupons**, I'll save about $20. That's a lot!"

Mayra / San Jose, California

"I make a shopping list. We're on a **budget**, so we plan our meals every week. Before we go food shopping, we make a list of everything we need. If it isn't on the list, we don't buy it. This way, we only buy the food we need, nothing else!"

Linda and Tom / Portland, Oregon

"We shop at a **farmers' market** for fruits and vegetables. A small bag of lettuce at the supermarket costs almost $3. At the farmers' market, I can buy a large head of lettuce for $1.50. And everything's very fresh."

Jan and Chris / Miami, Florida

"I always buy the store brands. At my supermarket, the store brand products are usually on the shelf next to the **name brand products**. They have the same ingredients as the name brands and they taste the same. And they're a lot cheaper!"

Alberto / Houston, Texas

"I don't go food shopping when I'm hungry. If I shop on an empty stomach, I always buy too much food. I try to eat first. When I'm full, it's easier to say 'no' to **junk food** like potato chips and candy!"

Jiao / Fort Lee, New Jersey

CHECK YOUR UNDERSTANDING

A Read the article again. What is the main idea of the article?

a. There are many ways to save money on food.

b. Food prices are very high.

c. You spend more at the supermarket when you are hungry.

B Find the boldface words in the article. Guess the meaning of each word from the words or sentences around it. Write the meaning of each word on the line.

1. double coupons: _____

2. budget: _____

3. name-brand products: _____

4. farmers' market: _____

5. junk food: _____

C Play track 36. Listen and check your answers. Were your guesses in Exercise B correct?

D Read the article again. Answer the questions.

1. What does Mayra look for in the newspaper? How much can Mayra save?

_____

2. What do Linda and Tom take to the supermarket? Why do they take it?

_____

3. What does Alberto buy at the supermarket? Why does he buy them?

_____

4. Where do Jan and Chris shop? Why do they shop there?

_____

5. What does Jiao do before she goes to the supermarket? Why does she do that?

_____

E MAKE IT PERSONAL. Where do you shop for food? How do you save money on food?

_____

_____

A **Complete the conversation. Underline the correct words.**

Waitress: Are you ready to order?

Ingrid: We need **a little** / (a few) more minutes.

Waitress: No problem. Can I answer **any** / **a lot of** questions about the menu?

Ingrid: Do you have **any** / **a little** fish?

Waitress: We have a fish sandwich. It's here, in the list of lunch specials.

Ingrid: Sounds good. I'd like that.

Waitress: Would you like **many** / **some** French fries with that?

Ingrid: Could I get **any** / **some** coleslaw instead?

Waitress: Of course. And for you, sir?

Allen: I'd like the roast chicken.

Waitress: Would you like **any** / **a lot of** sides with that?

Allen: Mashed potatoes, please.

Waitress: Anything to drink?

Ingrid: I'll have some iced tea, with just **a little** / **a few** sugar.

Allen: **Any** / **Some** water for me, please.

Waitress: Sure. I'll be right back with your drinks.

B 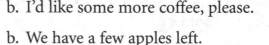 **Play track 37. Listen to the questions. Choose the correct responses.**

1. a. No, I need a little more time.　　　b. I'd like some more coffee, please.

2. a. Yes. We have apple and orange juice.　　b. We have a few apples left.

3. a. A hamburger and a side of coleslaw.　　b. I'll be right back with your order.

4. a. I'd like a soda, please.　　b. Some mixed vegetables, please.

5. a. A glass of milk, please.　　b. I'll have the fish.

C 🔘 Play track 38. Listen to customers ordering at a restaurant. Which guest check matches the customers' order? Circle the letter.

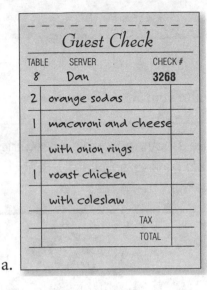

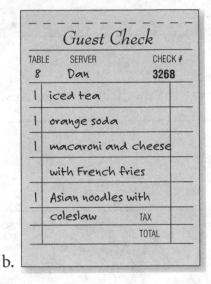

Guest Check		
TABLE	SERVER	CHECK #
8	Dan	3268
2	orange sodas	
1	macaroni and cheese	
	with onion rings	
1	roast chicken	
	with coleslaw	
	TAX	
	TOTAL	

a.

Guest Check		
TABLE	SERVER	CHECK #
8	Dan	3268
1	iced tea	
1	orange soda	
1	macaroni and cheese	
	with French fries	
1	Asian noodles with	
	coleslaw	TAX
		TOTAL

b.

Guest Check		
TABLE	SERVER	CHECK #
8	Dan	3268
2	orange sodas	
1	macaroni and cheese	
	with coleslaw	
1	roast chicken with	
	onion rings	
	TAX	
	TOTAL	

c.

D 🔘 Play track 39. Listen to a customer ordering at a restaurant. Write the customer's order on the guest check.

Guest Check		
TABLE	SERVER	CHECK #
		04421

E MAKE IT PERSONAL. What is your favorite restaurant? Why do you like it? What foods do you like to order?

_____

_____

_____

Lesson 1: Vocabulary

A Look at the pictures. What are the medical emergencies? Write sentences from the box.

> She's bleeding.
> He's having a heart attack.
> He swallowed poison.
>
> ~~He's choking.~~
> She's unconscious.
> She burned herself.
>
> She's having trouble breathing.
> He's having an allergic reaction.
> He fell.

1. *He's choking.*

2. _____

3. _____

4. _____

5. _____

6. _____

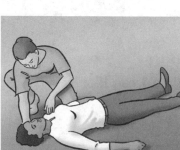

7. _____

8. _____

9. _____

B WORD PLAY. Complete the sentences. Match the beginnings and endings.

1. __c__ He's having a

2. _____ She's having trouble

3. _____ He swallowed

4. _____ He's having an

5. _____ She burned

a. breathing.

b. allergic reaction.

c. heart attack.

d. poison.

e. herself.

C Play track 40. Listen. Complete the conversations. Write the words you hear.

1. **A:** Would you like eggs for breakfast?

   B: No, I can't eat eggs. If I eat them, I have _____.

2. **A:** My grandfather went to the hospital this morning.

   B: Oh no. What's the matter?

   A: He had chest pains. He almost had _____.

3. **A:** Be careful with that knife.

   B: Ow!

   A: Uh-oh. Your finger is _____. Here, let me help you.

4. **A:** Is the soup hot?

   B: Yes, very hot. Don't _____. Let it cool.

5. **A:** There was an ambulance at the café.

   B: Really? What happened?

   A: A woman was _____. She had some food stuck in her throat.

D MAKE IT PERSONAL. Write about a time you or someone you know had a medical emergency. What happened?

_____

_____

A Complete the conversations. Use the present continuous.

1. **A:** Why _____ is _____ this little boy (**cry**) _____ crying _____?

   B: His elbow (**bleed**) _____.

2. **A:** _____ you (**feel**) _____ OK? You don't look well.

   B: I don't know what's wrong. I (**have**) _____ trouble breathing.

3. **A:** What (**happen**) _____ downtown?

   B: I'm not sure. There are a lot of fire trucks in the street.

4. **A:** _____ the fire trucks (**come**) _____?

   B: Yes, don't worry. I hear them now.

5. **A:** Why _____ he (**take**) _____ his son to the emergency room?

   B: His son ate some peanuts, and he (**have**) _____ an allergic reaction.

B Complete the conversation between a 911 caller and an operator. Use the verbs in the box. Change the verbs to the present continuous.

> call   happen   ~~have~~   lie   talk

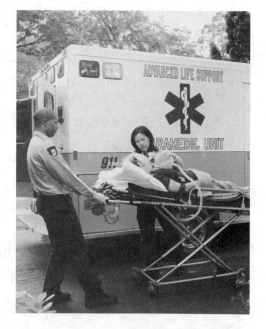

A: 9-1-1. What's your emergency?

B: It's my neighbor. She _'s having_ trouble breathing.

A: OK. Tell me what _____. Are you with

your neighbor now?

B: Yes, she _____ on the floor of my apartment.

A: Is she unconscious?

B: No, she's awake. My daughters _____ to her.

A: What's your location?

B: 180 Fifth Street. I _____ from Apartment 12 on the second floor.

C Unscramble the questions. Write the questions on the line.

1. (the / What's / emergency) _____

2. (woman / the / Is / bleeding) _____

3. (the / unconscious / woman / Is) _____

4. (the / of / What's / the / emergency / location) _____

5. (the / What / are / streets / cross) _____

6. (calling / Who / 911 / is) _____

7. (is / now / happening / What) _____

D Play track 41. Listen to the 911 call. Then answer the questions you wrote in Exercise C.

1. _A woman fell and hit her head._ _____

2. _____

3. _____

4. _____

5. _____

6. _____

7. _____

E MAKE IT PERSONAL. Have you or someone you know ever called 911 to report a medical emergency? What was the situation? What questions did the 911 operator ask?

_____

_____

A Play track 42. Listen to the conversation about fire hazards. Complete the fire safety tips. Write the words you hear.

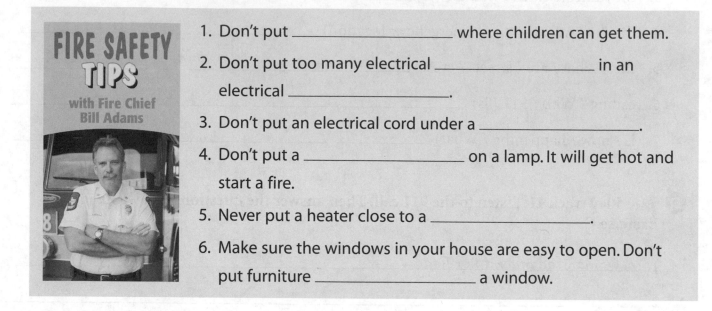

FIRE SAFETY TIPS

with Fire Chief Bill Adams

1. Don't put _____ where children can get them.

2. Don't put too many electrical _____ in an electrical _____.

3. Don't put an electrical cord under a _____.

4. Don't put a _____ on a lamp. It will get hot and start a fire.

5. Never put a heater close to a _____.

6. Make sure the windows in your house are easy to open. Don't put furniture _____ a window.

B Complete the sentences with the words in the box.

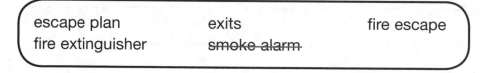

escape plan   exits   fire escape
fire extinguisher   ~~smoke alarm~~

1. A _____smoke alarm_____ protects you from fire when you are sleeping. It makes a loud noise when there is smoke in the air.

2. It is important to know the location of doors, windows, and stairs. These are the _____ of a building.

3. A _____ is a metal container with water or chemicals in it. You use it to stop a small fire.

4. Many buildings with two or more floors have a _____ on the outside of the building. These stairs lead from a window to the ground.

5. An _____ is a map of a building. It shows how to exit in case of a fire.

C Look at the map of the Yang family's apartment. Draw an escape plan for the Yang family. Draw arrows to show all of the exits in each room.

YANG FAMILY ESCAPE PLAN

D MAKE IT PERSONAL. Make an escape plan for your family. Draw a map of your home. Draw arrows to show all of the exits in each room. Choose a family meeting place outside of your home, such as a neighbor's house, a mailbox, or a parking lot.

MY FAMILY ESCAPE PLAN

FAMILY MEETING PLACE: _____

Lessons 5–6: Describe an emergency

A Look at the pictures. Write the dangerous situations. Use the words in the box.

> a car accident   a construction accident   an explosion   a robbery

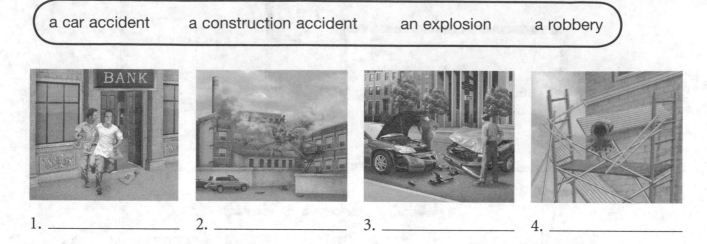

1. _____   2. _____   3. _____   4. _____

B Look at the news website. Complete the sentences with *there* and *was* or *were*.

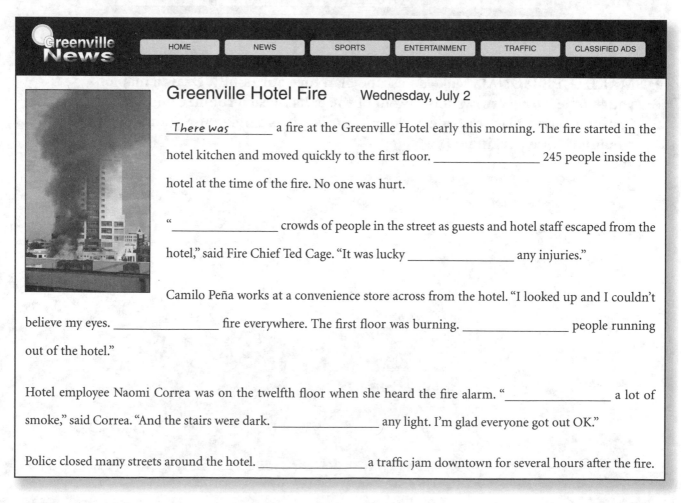

Greenville News   HOME   NEWS   SPORTS   ENTERTAINMENT   TRAFFIC   CLASSIFIED ADS

Greenville Hotel Fire   Wednesday, July 2

_There was_____ a fire at the Greenville Hotel early this morning. The fire started in the hotel kitchen and moved quickly to the first floor. _____ 245 people inside the hotel at the time of the fire. No one was hurt.

"_____ crowds of people in the street as guests and hotel staff escaped from the hotel," said Fire Chief Ted Cage. "It was lucky _____ any injuries."

Camilo Peña works at a convenience store across from the hotel. "I looked up and I couldn't believe my eyes. _____ fire everywhere. The first floor was burning. _____ people running out of the hotel."

Hotel employee Naomi Correa was on the twelfth floor when she heard the fire alarm. "_____ a lot of smoke," said Correa. "And the stairs were dark. _____ any light. I'm glad everyone got out OK."

Police closed many streets around the hotel. _____ a traffic jam downtown for several hours after the fire.

C Look at the pictures on the TV news. Describe the emergency situations.
Write sentences with *there* and *was* or *were*.

1. CAR ACCIDENT ON 7TH AVENUE

2. MANY INJURIES REPORTED

3.

4. GAS TRUCK EXPLOSION INJURES 2 FIREFIGHTERS

5.

6. TRAFFIC JAM DOWNTOWN

1. There was a car accident on Seventh Avenue.

2. _____

3. _____

4. _____

5. _____

6. _____

READ

Play track 43. Listen. Read the newspaper article.

LOCAL HERO RESCUES FAMILY

A Greenville man rescued three people from a car that crashed into Jordan Lake Saturday morning.

Miguel Torres, 34, was fishing at the lake at 6:30 A.M. He saw a car drive off the road and into the lake.

"I didn't think," said Torres, "I just jumped into the water. I knew those people needed help fast."

Torres swam to the car, and his son, Jamie, 12, called 911. The water was at the height of the car doors. Torres tried to open the doors, but he couldn't open them. He could see three people inside the car: Tom and Marcia Tully, 42, and their ten-year-old son Alan. They were all hurt and unconscious.

"I found a metal pipe, and I hit the window until it broke. I carried the boy out of the water," said Torres. "I went back for the mother and then the father. The man was a big guy, over six feet tall and heavy. But I just picked him up. I don't know how I did it."

"When I arrived at the accident, the car was totally underwater," said Greenville police officer Rick Adams. "Miguel Torres saved that family. He's a hero."

"I'm really proud of my dad," said Jamie Torres. "He's actually afraid of water. He's a poor swimmer. He was really brave."

Miguel Torres disagrees that he did anything special. "Anybody would do what I did. I just happened to be there. In fact, we almost went home early. It was raining. We just wanted to catch one more fish. It's lucky the fishing was bad that day!"

CHECK YOUR UNDERSTANDING

A Read the article again. What is the subject of the article?

a. There was a car accident on Fox Road.

b. Three people were injured.

c. A man rescued three people from a car in Jordan Lake.

B Look at the pictures of the accident at Jordan Lake. Number the pictures in the order they happened. Then write sentences to describe each picture.

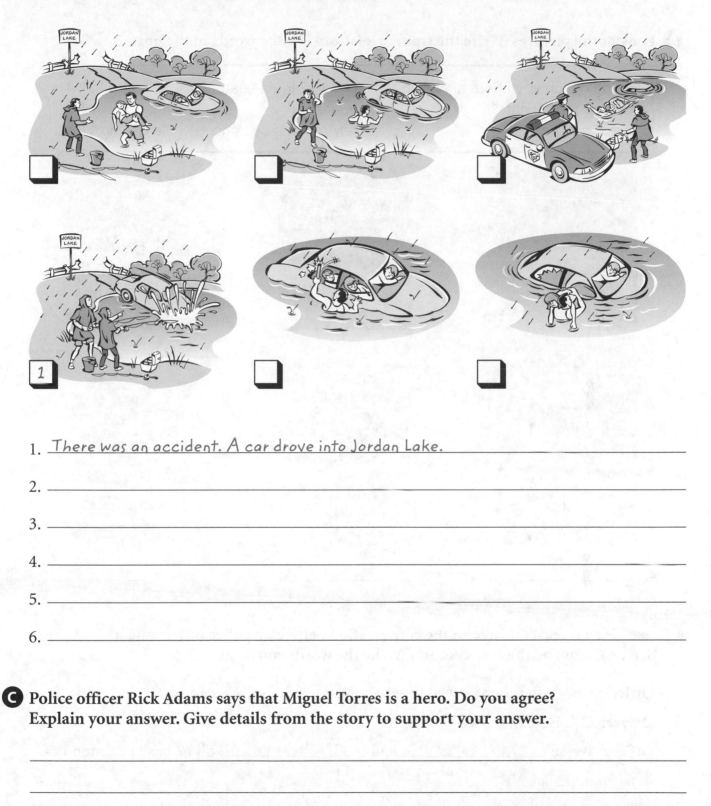

1. _There was an accident. A car drove into Jordan Lake._

2. _____

3. _____

4. _____

5. _____

6. _____

C Police officer Rick Adams says that Miguel Torres is a hero. Do you agree? Explain your answer. Give details from the story to support your answer.

_____

_____

_____

A Look at the pictures. Write the traffic violation. Use the words in the box.

> changing lanes without signaling   not wearing a seatbelt
> running a red light   ~~speeding~~
> tailgating   talking on a cell phone while driving

1. _____speeding_____

2. _____

3. _____

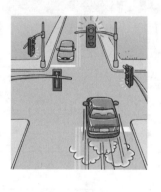

4. _____

5. _____

6. _____

B 🖸 Play track 44. Listen to the conversation between a police officer and a driver. Complete the conversation. Write the words you hear.

Officer: Good afternoon. I need to see your _____ and _____.

Driver: OK. Here they are.

Officer: Please _____ and _____. I'll be back in a moment.

[a few minutes later]

Officer: Sir, I pulled you over for _____. I'm giving you a _____ this time. Please drive safely.

C Read the advice about ways to save money on gas. Then combine two imperatives in bold with *and* or *or*.

Dos and Don'ts for Saving Money on Gas

Would you like to save money on gas? If your answer is yes, prepare to change the way you drive. Small changes can save you big money at the gas station. Here are a few tips for the road.

Dos

Drive slower. You will use 23 percent less gas if you drive 55 miles per hour instead of 75 miles per hour.

Stay at the same speed. You use more gas when you change speeds often.

Maintain your engine. You will use less gas if your engine is working correctly. Follow the maintenance schedule in your car's owner's manual.

Check the air in your tires. If your tires have too much or too little air, you use more gas. Check them every two weeks.

Turn off the engine. If you have to wait for more than two minutes, turn off the engine and save gas.

Empty your trunk. Heavier cars use more gas than lighter cars. Take everything out of the car that you don't need. Keep your extra tire, though!

Don'ts

Don't start or stop quickly. When you get a green light at traffic light, don't try to speed up too quickly. Fast stops and starts use more gas.

Don't get stuck in traffic. If you can, avoid driving when there is a lot of traffic. Try to plan trips for when there are fewer cars on the road.

Don't run just one errand. Run many errands at the same time. You can save time and gas!

Don't use the air-conditioning. Use the air-conditioning only when you need it. If it's not that hot, keep it off and save gas.

---

1. _Drive slower and stay at the same speed._ _____

2. _____

3. _____

4. _____

5. _____

D MAKE IT PERSONAL. Do you know someone who is a good or bad driver? Explain why you think so.

_____

_____

Unit 12: The World of Work

Lesson 1: Vocabulary

A WORD PLAY. Complete the job responsibilities. Match the words. Write the letters on the lines.

1. _b_ wear   a. hands

2. ____ maintain   b. latex gloves

3. ____ wash   c. the equipment

4. ____ ask   d. late

5. ____ call in   e. in / out

6. ____ clock   f. questions

B Look at the pictures. Write the job responsibilities from Exercise A.

1. _____   2. _____   3. _____

4. _____   5. _____   6. _____

C 🔘 **Play track 45. Listen to the employees talk about their job responsibilities. Match the employees with their jobs.**

1. _____ Nina

2. _____ Anthony

3. _____ Leona

a food service worker

a housekeeper

a construction worker

D **Look at the pictures. What are each worker's job responsibilities? Write a list.**

a waitress

a gardner

a nurse

ask questions		

A Look at the signs. Complete the statements. Use *must, must not, have to,* or *can't* and a verb from the box. Some verbs may be used more than once.

enter	make	park	smoke	wash	wear

1. All warehouse employees ____<u>must wear</u>____ work boots. Warehouse

   employees _____ sneakers.

2. Employees _____ outside the building in the smoking area.

   They _____ in the break room.

3. Employees _____ in the employee parking area. Employees

   _____ in the customer parking area.

4. All employees _____ an ID badge. Non-employees

   _____ this area.

5. Employees _____ personal calls at work. They

   _____ calls at lunch time or during breaks.

6. All employees _____ their hands after using the restroom.

7. Employees _____ safety gear in this area at all times.

BE SAFE
WEAR
WORK BOOTS

NO SMOKING
IN THE BUILDING

Employee
parking only →

Visitor
parking only ←

Employees
with
ID
only

No calls
on work time

Wash your hands
before returning
to work.

Safety gear
required

B 🔘 Play track 46. Listen to company policies for the Greenville Café. Complete the sentences with the words you hear.

☕ *Greenville Café*   **Company Policies**

Welcome to the Greenville Café! Below is a list of our company policies. If you have any questions, please ask your supervisor.

1. Employees ____*must park*____ behind the restaurant in the employee parking lot.

2. Employees _____ in or out for other employees.

3. Employees _____ a uniform: a white shirt and black pants.

4. Employees _____ breaks at a scheduled time.

5. Employees _____ a food safety class.

6. Employees _____ to an employee meeting every month.

7. Employees _____ their schedules every Monday.

8. Employees _____ for work more than three times.

C Look at the picture. Greg is a new employee at the Greenville Café. What are Greg's responsibilities? Write sentences with *must, must not, have to,* and *can't.*

1. _Greg has to clock in and out._

2. _____

3. _____

4. _____

A Look at Viet's pay stub. Match the information on the pay stub with the definitions. Write the letter on the line.

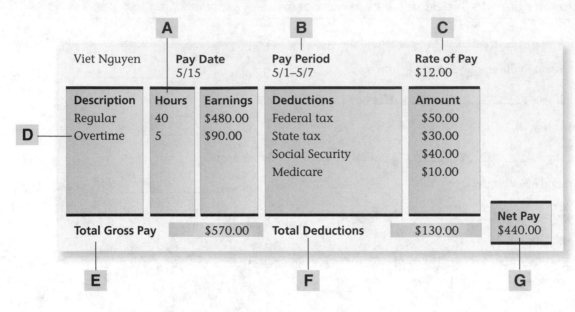

1. __B__ days Viet worked for this paycheck

2. _____ number of hours Viet worked

3. _____ money Viet got before taxes

4. _____ overtime hours Viet worked

5. _____ money taken out to pay for taxes and insurance

6. _____ money Viet makes per hour

7. _____ money Viet got after taxes

B Look at Viet's pay stub in Exercise A. Complete the sentences.

1. Viet's gross pay is __$570.00__.

2. Viet is paid _____ per hour.

3. Viet worked five hours of _____.

4. Viet's net pay is _____.

5. Viet worked a total of _____ hours.

6. Viet's total deductions are _____.

7. Viet got paid on _____.

8. Viet's federal tax was _____.

C Look at Claudia's pay stub. Answer Claudia's questions.

Claudia Esteban		Pay Date 11/15		Pay Period 11/1–11/14	Rate of Pay $8.50
Description	**Hours**	**Earnings**	**Deductions**		**Amount**
Regular	40	$340.00	Federal tax		$35.00
Overtime	6	$ 76.50	Soc. Sec.		$20.00
			Medicare		$10.00
Total Gross Pay		$416.50	**Total Deductions**	$55.00	**Net Pay** $361.50

Claudia

How much money did I get paid per hour?

How much did I get paid per hour for overtime?

How many overtime hours did I work?

1. _____

2. _____

3. _____

What is this $20.00 deduction for?

When I cash this check, how much money will I get?

Is this for one week of work?

4. _____

5. _____

6. _____

D Read about each worker's schedule and pay. Then look at the pay stubs. Circle the mistake on each worker's pay stub.

Ibrahim

I worked 40 hours. I get paid $14 per hour.

Description	Hours	Rate of Pay	Earnings
Regular	30	$14.00	$490.00

Carlos

I worked 45 hours. I get paid $7.50 per hour.

Description	Hours	Rate of Pay	Earnings
Regular	40	$7.50	$300.00
Overtime	5	$7.50	$ 37.50

A Complete the conversations. Write questions with *Who, What time, Which,*
Where and the words in parentheses. Capitalize the first word.

1. **A:** (work) <u>Who worked</u> last weekend?

   B: I think Eric worked on Saturday and Marta worked on Sunday.

2. **A:** (my shift / begin) _____ tomorrow?

   B: At 9:30 A.M. You and Mike are opening the store.

3. **A:** (you / call) _____ about trading shifts?

   B: I called Mike. He said he could work my shift on Friday.

4. **A:** (shift, prefer) _____, morning or evening?

   B: I prefer the morning shift. I have to be home with my children at night.

5. **A:** (work) _____ on Saturdays?

   B: At a warehouse. I work there part-time on weekends.

6. **A:** (store, close) _____ tonight?

   B: The store closes at 9 P.M., but you need to stay until 10:00 to help clean up.

B Play track 47. Listen to the conversations. Write the question that you
hear in each conversation. Then listen again. Answer the questions.

1. Question: <u>Who do I talk to about my schedule?</u>

   Answer: <u>Walter, the assistant manager.</u>

2. Question: _____

   Answer: _____

3. Question: _____

   Answer: _____

4. Question: _____

   Answer: _____

C **Complete the conversations. Ask about the underlined information. Write information questions with *Who, What time, When, Which,* and *Where*.**

1. **A:** _Which days do you have off?_

   B: I have Friday and Sunday off.

2. **A:** _____

   B: I usually take my break at 3:30.

3. **A:** _____

   B: Daniel traded shifts with me today. I'm going to work for him tomorrow.

4. **A:** _____

   B: Store the safety gear in the cabinet. You can't take it home.

5. **A:** _____

   B: I need time off on Monday and Tuesday. I need to visit my mother in the hospital.

D **Read the work schedule. Answer the questions.**

	Mon.	Tues.	Wed.	Thu.	Fri.	Sat.	Sun.
Viktor, cashier	OFF	7–3 Break: 10–11	7–3 Break: 10–11	7–3 Break: 10–11	7–3 Break: 10–11	7–3 Break: 10–11	OFF
Ana, cashier	OFF	OFF	8–4 Break: 2–3	8–4 Break: 2–3	8–4 Break: 2–3	8–4 Break: 2–3	8–4 Break: 2–3
Franco, grocery department	OFF	10–6 Break: 2–3	10–6 Break: 2–3	10–6 Break: 2–3	OFF	10–6 Break: 2–3	10–6 Break: 2–3

1. What time does Viktor start work?

   _At 7:00 A.M._

2. When does Ana take a break? _____

3. Which days does Franco have off?

   _____

4. What time does Ana get off work? _____

5. Who works on Friday? _____

   _____

6. Who doesn't work on Friday? _____

7. Where does Franco work? _____

8. Which employee has Sunday off?

   _____

BEFORE YOU READ

Look at the title of the article and the picture. Think about what you already know about the topic. What is important for success at work? Write three tips.

1. _____   2. _____   3. _____

READ

Play track 48. Listen. Read the article.

Tips for Success at Work

Have you ever noticed that some people have a talent for doing well at work? These co-workers always seem to get ahead. They get the best work schedules and the most overtime hours. They get promoted quickly to positions with better pay and more responsibilities. Want to learn the secrets of these star employees? Being successful at work is more than just completing your job duties. Here are five tips for workplace success.

1. Know your responsibilities. Make sure you understand what your supervisor expects you to do. Don't be afraid to ask questions if you don't understand your work assignments. It's better to ask questions than to waste time doing your job wrong.

2. Get along with your co-workers. Be friendly and treat your co-workers with respect. Give your co-workers a hand when they need help. Offer to train new employees.

3. Stay busy. If you finish your work early, find something else to do. For example, use the time to clean up your area or store your equipment. Don't wait for the boss to tell you what to do. If you see something that needs to be done, go ahead and do it.

4. Learn from your mistakes. Nobody likes to be told they are doing something wrong, but try to see this as a chance to learn something. Ask your supervisor for suggestions on how you can do better next time.

5. Look for ways to learn new skills. Volunteer for company training programs. Ask other workers to show you how to do things. Don't be afraid to try new things.

CHECK YOUR UNDERSTANDING

A **Read the article again. What is the purpose of the article?**

a. to help people become successful at work

b. to show that some employees are given better schedules than others

c. to help people get along with their co-workers

B **Complete the tips with information from the article.**

1. Don't be afraid to _____ if you don't understand your _____.

2. Give your _____ a hand when they need _____.

3. If you _____ your work early, _____ something else to do.

4. Ask your _____ for suggestions on how you can do better _____.

5. Don't be _____ to _____ new things.

C **Read about the employees. Match each employee's behavior with one of the five tips from the article. Write the number of the tip on the line.**

1. ____ Kyle got a job as a stock clerk in a drug store. On his first day, his supervisor told him to stock aisle 3. Kyle wasn't sure how to find the price for each item. He went back to his supervisor and asked for help.

2. ____ Gennette is a food service worker at a cafeteria. Her boss asked her to prepare the food in the salad bar. After she finished, she noticed that many of the tables were dirty. She took a wet towel and cleaned the tables.

3. ____ Anita is an office assistant. This week, her company will give a class on how to use a new computer program. Anita isn't good with computers, so she enrolled in the course. She thinks it will help her be a better employee.

4. ____ Anthony works in a warehouse. Yesterday, Anthony's supervisor told him that he was working too slowly. At first, Anthony was embarrassed and angry. But then he asked his supervisor for advice. His supervisor gave him some tips and now Anthony is doing better.

5. ____ Myung-Hee started working at the Greenville Café four years ago. Last week, a new waitress named Kim started working at the café. Myung-Hee introduced Kim to all of the other workers. She showed her how to clock in and helped her when she had questions.

A Complete the conversations. Put the words in order. Write questions with *Can* or *Could.*

1. **A:** (I / Can / to you / for a moment / talk) _Can I talk to you for a moment?_

   B: Of course. What's up?

2. **A:** (cover / Could / next Saturday / you / my shift) _____

   B: Sure. I need the extra money.

3. **A:** (you / store the equipment / Could / help me) _____

   B: OK, I'll be there in five minutes.

4. **A:** (ask you / I / about taking some vacation time / Can) _____

   B: Well, Ms. Mills usually handles vacation requests.

5. **A:** (I / change / to evenings / Could) _____

   B: I'm not sure. I'll look at the schedule next week and see what I can do.

B 🔘 Play track 49. Listen. Complete the conversations with the words you hear.

1. **Bae:** Hi, Kristen. _____ to you for a minute?

   Kristen: Of course. What's up?

   Bae: _____ work a little early on Thursday? My son is graduating from kindergarten at 4:00.

   Kristen: Well, _____ a little later this afternoon?

   Bae: Yes, I _____. No problem.

2. **Miguel:** _____ on Saturday, Angelica?

   Angelica: Well, I take my children to swim class on Saturday mornings.

   Miguel: _____ Saturday afternoon? Janet is out sick and I need someone to cover her hours.

   Angelica: Sure. _____ at 1:00?

   Miguel: That's great. Thanks.

C Rewrite the underlined sentences to ask permission. Change the imperative statements to questions with *Can* or *Could*.

1. I don't know what this word means. <u>Give me your dictionary.</u>

   Could I borrow your dictionary?

2. I have to take my wife to the doctor. <u>Let me have the morning off.</u>

   _____

3. I really want to make some extra money. <u>Give me some overtime hours next week.</u>

   _____

4. Excuse me. <u>I need to ask you something.</u>

   _____

5. I want to take some time off. <u>Cover my hours this weekend.</u>

   _____

6. It isn't time for my break, but I want to get something to eat. <u>Let me take a break early.</u>

   _____

D Read the situations. You need to ask your supervisor for permission. What can you say? Write questions with *Can* or *Could*.

1. You work as a security guard at night. You have to go to a parent-teacher conference next Wednesday night. You want the night off.

   Could I have next Wednesday night off?

2. You want to take classes in the evenings. You want to change to the morning shift.

   _____

3. You are working until 3:30 today. You need to pick up your son at school at 4:00. You want to leave 15 minutes early.

   _____

4. You work in store. You want to take some classes in the morning. You need evening hours.

   _____

Unit 1, Page 5, Exercise C

Jack: Hey, Paul. Are you coming to my house for dinner tonight?

Paul: Yeah, thanks for inviting me, Jack.

Jack: I'm inviting Carol, too.

Paul: Carol?

Jack: You know—she has short, curly blond hair.

Paul: Oh. She has blue eyes, right?

Jack: No, she doesn't have blue eyes. She has brown eyes.

Paul: Hmmm. Is she tall?

Jack: Yes, she is. And she's slim.

Paul: Oh, Carol! I know who you're talking about now. She's very pretty.

Jack: Yeah, and she wants to meet you!

Unit 2, Page 17, Exercise D

A: Where is Roberta?

B: She's at work. She has a new job.

A: Really? Where?

B: She works in a department store.

A: Is it a good job?

B: It's OK. She lives near the store. And the hours are good. She works from 7:30 A.M. to 3:00 P.M.

A: That's good.

B: Yeah. She can take care of her kids when they get home from school.

A: Does her husband still work in a hospital?

B: Yes, he does. He's doing well there.

Unit 2, Page 21, Exercise C

A: Hi, Phil. How are you?

B: I'm sorry, I'm not Phil. I'm Ben. I'm . . .

A: Wow, you look like my friend Phil! You have red hair and Phil does, too.

B: Yes, I'm . . .

A: And Phil lives here in Las Vegas.

B: And I do, too. You see, I'm . . .

A: Do you work for a computer company?

B: Yes, I'm . . .

A: Phil does, too. Do your parents live in Las Vegas?

B: No, they don't.

A: Phil's parents' don't, either. They live in Ohio.

B: I know they live in Ohio. You see, I'm Phil's brother. His twin brother!

Unit 2, Page 23, Exercise C

A: I'd like to mail this package.

B: OK. How do you want to send it?

A: Can I send it First Class?

B: No, I'm sorry. The package must be 13 ounces or less for First Class. You can send it Parcel Post.

A: How long does Parcel Post take?

B: Two to nine days.

A: That's fine. I'll send it Parcel Post.

B: All right. Do you need any extra services?

A: Delivery Confirmation, please.

Unit 3, Page 33, Exercise C

Irene: I can't wait for Jeff's birthday party tonight! Do I need to bring anything?

Cindy: Well, let's see. Scott is going to get some ice cream on his way home from work. Alex and Nina are going to bring pizza and soda. I'm going to bake a cake.

Irene: Did you remember the decorations?

Cindy: Yes. My sister is going to buy balloons and party games.

Irene: Cake, ice cream, pizza, games . . . sounds like it's going to be a fun party!

Cindy: Oh no! I need to go to the store.

Irene: Why?

Cindy: I forgot something very important. I forgot to buy Jeff's birthday present!

Unit 3, Page 36, Exercise C

1. **A:** I need to return these pants.
   B: Why? What's wrong with them?
   A: Look. They're the wrong size.
   B: Wow. They ARE very big!
2. **A:** Can I help you?
   B: Yes, please. I need to return this jacket.
   A: OK. Is there a problem with the jacket?
   B: Yes, there's a hole in the pocket.
3. **A:** Are you going to wear your new shirt?
   B: I can't wear it.
   A: Why not?
   B: It's too tight and a seam is ripped.
4. **A:** I like your new raincoat.
   B: Thanks. I really like it, too. But I need to exchange it.
   A: Why? It fits you well.
   B: I know. But a button is missing.
   A: Oh, too bad.
5. **A:** What are you doing?
   B: I'm going to the store. I need to return these boots.
   A: How come?
   B: They're too tight. They hurt my feet.

Unit 4, Page 43, Exercise C

1. **A:** Greenville Community Center. May I help you?
   B: Uh, hi. Do you have any dance classes?
   A: Dance classes? Yes, we do.
   B: When are they?
   A: Let's see . . . the dance class meets the first and third Monday of the Month from 7:00 to 9:00 P.M.
2. **A:** Excuse me. My friend needs to learn English. Do you have any classes?
   B: Let me check. . . . Yes, we do have an English class.
   A: Great! When is it?
   B: On Tuesday and Thursday evenings.
   A: What time?
   B: It meets from 5:30 to 7:00 P.M.
3. **A:** Look. There's a new swimming class.
   B: When is it?
   A: Wednesdays at 4 o'clock.
   B: And when does it end?
   A: 6 o'clock.
   B: Great. We should sign the kids up.
4. **A:** Hey. It says here that there is a Walking Club at the community center. It meets every Sunday. We should go.
   B: Well, I do need some exercise. What time does it meet?
   A: Let's see. . . . It meets from 7:00 to 8:00 A.M.
   B: Seven o'clock in the morning . . . on a Sunday!? No way!
5. **A:** Want to see a movie tomorrow? The community center has a free movie night.
   B: Sounds like fun. When is it?
   A: Every Saturday night at 7:30.
   B: Let's go!

Unit 4, Page 45, Exercise C

1. **Rick:** Hi, Angie.
   Angie: Hi, Rick. Hey, let's do something on Saturday.
   Rick: Sure. Do you want to go hiking? I love hiking.
   Angie: Hiking? I don't know. I don't really like to go hiking. How about going to the beach?
   Rick: To be honest, I hate to go to the beach. There are too many people. And I can't swim!
2. **Liz:** Let's go out to eat tonight. There's a new Italian restaurant. I heard it's good and not expensive.
   Fred: Sounds great. I love Italian food.
   Liz: Me, too. And we can go dancing after dinner. I love to dance.
   Fred: Me? Go dancing? No thanks.
   Liz: Oh, come on! It'll be fun!
   Fred: No way. I hate to dance

Unit 5, Page 56, Exercise A

Jackie: Hello?
Charlie: Hi, Jackie. This is Charlie at Richmond Realty. I have a nice apartment to show you.
Jackie: Great! Tell me about it.
Charlie: Well, it's really nice. There are three bedrooms. And there's a large living room.
Jackie: How many bathrooms are there?
Charlie: Two.
Jackie: Is there a dining room?
Charlie: There's no dining room, but there's a big eat-in kitchen.
Jackie: Sounds good. How's the location? Is there a park nearby?
Charlie: Yes, there is. Right around the corner.
Jackie: And is the neighborhood quiet?
Charlie: Yes, it's on a very quite street. There isn't a lot of traffic.
Jackie: Wow. That sounds perfect. Can I see it today?

Unit 5, Page 61, Exercise B

1. **A:** I need directions to the library.
   B: OK. At the stop sign, turn left. Then go through two traffic lights.
   A: Thanks.
2. **A:** Excuse me. Where's the post office?
   B: Go straight. It's on this street.
   A: Thanks very much.
3. **A:** Where's the pharmacy?
   B: At the traffic light, turn left. It's on the right.
   A: Thank you.
4. **A:** How do I get to the coffee shop?
   B: Go through two traffic lights. The coffee shop is on the left.
   A: Thanks a lot.
5. **A:** Is there a Chinese restaurant near here?
   B: Yes. Go straight on Pine Street. Go through one traffic light and turn left.
   A: Great!

Unit 5, Page 61, Exercise C

A: Can you give me directions to the hospital?
B: Sure. Go straight on Miller Street.
A: OK. Go straight on Miller Street.
B: Then go through two traffic lights.
A: Go through two traffic lights.
B: Yes. Then turn left onto Ventura Avenue.
A: Turn left onto Ventura Avenue.
B: Exactly. Then go through three stop signs.
A: Go through three stop signs.
B: Yes. The hospital is on the right.
A: Got it. Thanks!

Unit 6, Page 63, Exercise C

1. **A:** Wow. All of this food looks delicious. Did you bring the chicken?
   B: No, I think John and Mary brought the chicken. I brought the potato soup.
   A: Mmmm. I can't wait to try it!
2. **A:** Mr. Wang, you've worked for this company for 30 years. We're all going to miss you.
   B: Thank you. Thank you very much.
   A: Do you have any plans for the future?
   B: Well, I'm going to go fishing next week.
3. **A:** Is David coming?
   B: Yes, he's almost here.
   A: He thinks he's coming to see a football game.
   B: There he is! Ssssh!
   All: Surprise!
4. **A:** Hi, Aunt Martha.
   B: Oh my goodness! Little Johnny! You aren't little anymore!
   A: No, the last time I saw you, I was 10. Now I'm 20.
   B: Look—There are my cousins Joe and Rita! Oh, it's so nice to see everyone again.

Unit 6, Page 64, Exercise B

Rich: How was the family reunion?
Ann: Very nice. We all missed you.
Rich: Yeah. I was sorry I couldn't go. Who was there?
Ann: The whole family showed up. All the aunts, uncles, and cousins.
Rich: Aunt Lucy, too?
Ann: Of course. Everyone listened to her family stories. And we looked at old photos and watched movies of Grandma and Grandpa's wedding.
Rich: Oh yeah? I'm sorry I missed that!
Ann: Well, you should have come! We had a great time. We stayed up late and talked all night.
Rich: Really? I'll definitely have to go next time!

Unit 6, Page 72, Exercise B

Jason had a bad day last Monday. On Sunday night, he stayed up late to watch a movie on TV. He was really tired, so he overslept on Monday morning. Jason got up and got dressed quickly. His wife gave him his lunch, and he ran out the door. But he forgot his wallet. When he got to the bus stop, he didn't have any money for the bus. He ran back to his apartment. He got his wallet and ran out the door again. This time he forgot his lunch. When he got to the bus stop, he jumped on the bus. But he took the wrong bus. He needed to take the number 5 bus, but he took the number 33 bus. He got off the bus and walked to work. When Jason finally got to work, it was 9:45. He was 45 minutes late. At lunch time, Jason was very hungry. He didn't have his lunch, so he went to the candy machine. He put a dollar into the machine, but nothing happened. He lost his money. Jason had to stay late. He had a lot of work to finish. He got home at 7:30. He was hungry and exhausted. He decided that he would stop staying up late on Sunday nights!

Unit 7, Page 75, Exercise C

Dear Grandma,
We are on vacation this week. Last weekend, we went camping at a state park. We did NOT have a good time. Dad cooked on the campfire every night. The food was really bad. Dad had heartburn and I had an upset stomach. On Saturday, it rained all day. Mom got sick. She had a sore throat and a cough. On Sunday, Janet and I went swimming. Janet got water in her ear. Now she has an earache. Then Dad and I went hiking. Now I have a rash on my arms and legs. This morning we went to a hotel. No more camping for us!
Love, Marie

Unit 7, Page 79, Exercise D

Pharmacist: Mr. Bronson, your prescription is ready. Is this the first time you are taking Naproxen?
Mr. Bronson: Yes, it is. How much do I take?
Pharmacist: Take two tablets three times a day.
Mr. Bronson: Do I take them with food?
Pharmacist: Yes. Take the tablets at breakfast, lunch, and dinner.
Mr. Bronson: And how long do I take them?
Pharmacist: Ten days.
Mr. Bronson: All right.
Pharmacist: This medicine can make you feel dizzy or nauseous. If this happens, stop taking the medicine and call your doctor.
Mr. Bronson: OK.
Pharmacist: Do you understand these directions?
Mr. Bronson: Yes, I do. Thank you.

Unit 8, Page 92, Exercise B

Julia came to the U.S. in January, 2004. A month later, she enrolled in an English class. In October, she started nursing classes at the community college. She graduated from nursing school two months ago.

Jung-Woo came to the U.S. in 2006. A year later, he got a job as a waiter in a restaurant. Two years ago, Jung-Woo got a better job. He is the assistant manager of a hotel.

Unit 8, Page 96, Exercise B

1. **A:** Can you work weekends?
   B: Yes, I'm available on Saturdays and Sundays.
   A: We really need someone for both days.
   B: I can do that.
2. **A:** Can you work first shift or second shift?
   B: When is first shift?
   A: First shift is from 8:00 A.M. to 3:00 P.M.
   B: That's perfect. I need to be home when my kids get out of school at 4 o'clock.
3. **A:** We need servers for the breakfast shift and the lunch shift. Can you start at 6 A.M.?
   B: No, I can't. I have to take my children to school. But I can work the lunch shift.
4. **A:** Can you work Monday through Friday?
   B: Yes, I can.
   A: How about weekends?
   B: No, I can't work weekends. I have another job on weekends.
   A: Do you prefer days or evenings?
   B: I prefer days but I can work evenings, too.

Unit 9, Page 101, Exercise C

Good morning, students. We have a busy week at Greenville Middle School. The Music Club will have a bake sale today. Club members will sell cookies and other baked goods from 11:30 to 12:30 in the cafeteria. The Technology Club will meet in the library today at 4:00. Bad news, Greenville basketball fans. There won't be a basketball game on Wednesday. The Greenville Tigers will play their next home game on Monday at 7:00 P.M. Don't forget there will be a Back-to-school Night for parents on Thursday at 7:30. Your parents will visit your classes and meet your teachers . . . but they won't do your homework for you! And finally, on Friday, the seventh grade class will take a field trip to the Greenville Science Museum. Please remember to bring a bag lunch. Thank you and have a good day.

Unit 9, Page 102, Exercise B

1. Good morning, Greenville High School.
2. May I speak to David Valenti, please?
3. May I take message?
4. Please ask Mr. James to call me back.
5. Can I have your telephone number?

Unit 9, Page 103, Exercise C

A: Good morning, Centerville High School.
B: May I speak to Mrs. Clemens please?
A: She's in class right now. May I take a message?
B: Yes, please. This is Roberto Santiago. My son Enrique needs some extra help with his science project. Can you ask her to call me back?
A: What's your number?
B: It's 718-555-4343.
A: OK, I'll give her the message.
B: Thank you, very much.

Unit 9, Page 103, Exercise D

A: Good morning, Redwood Middle School.
B: Hello. This is Maria Rodriguez. My son Juan Alonso is in first grade.
A: Oh yes. In Mrs. Miller's class.
B: Yes. Is Mrs. Miller available?
A: I'm sorry. She's in class right now. May I take a message?
B: Yes, please ask her to call me. I have a question about Juan's science fair project.
A: Sure. What's your telephone number?
B: My number is 718-555-4567.
A: OK, I'll give her the message.
B: Thank you.

Unit 10, Page 113, Exercise D

Paulo: I'm going to the supermarket. Do we need anything for dinner?
Clara: Well. I think I'm going to make some soup. Could you get some chicken?
Paulo: Sure. How much chicken do you need?
Clara: Let me check the recipe. . . . I need a pound of chicken.
Paulo: OK. Anything else?
Clara: Let's see. Are there any carrots?
Paulo: Yes, there's a bunch of carrots in the refrigerator.
Clara: That's enough. Is there any olive oil?
Paulo: Yes, there's a bottle of olive oil in the cabinet.
Clara: Good. Are there any potatoes?
Paulo: Um. No, there aren't any. I'll get a pound of potatoes.

Unit 10, Page 116, Exercise B

1. **Angel:** Hey, Claudia. Let's buy some soup. It's three cans for a dollar.

   Claudia: Actually, Angel, I don't like canned soup. It has too much salt. It's not good for you.

   Angel: Yeah, but it's so convenient. You just open the can and heat it up.

   Claudia: No thanks. I'll make some homemade soup tonight. Forget the cans . . . and the salt.

2. **Sam:** Let's go out for pizza at The Italian Café.

   Ann: That place is so expensive! I have a pizza in the freezer. I'll make that.

   Sam: Frozen pizza? Come on, Ann! I hate the taste. I want fresh vegetables and cheese.

   Ann: OK, Sam. But you can pay the bill!

3. **Sally:** Hey, Evan. I've got an idea. Let's barbecue some chicken at your birthday party.

   Evan: I don't know, Sally. That's a lot of work. Let's just make sandwiches. It's easier.

   Sally: Well, that's true, but barbecued chicken is really tasty.

Unit 10, Page 119, Exercise C

1. double coupons: when a store pays twice the value of any coupons you bring in
2. budget: a plan for how to save money
3. name-brand products: popular and well-known products
4. farmers' market: a place where local farmers sell their products
5. junk food: food that is not healthy because it contains a lot of oil or sugar

Unit 10, Page 120, Exercise B

1. Are you ready to order?
2. Do you have any fruit juice?
3. What can I get for you?
4. Any sides with that?
5. Can I get you something to drink?

Unit 10, Page 121, Exercise C

Waitress: Here are your orange sodas. Are you ready to order?

Soo-Jung: Yes, I'll have the macaroni and cheese.

Waitress: OK. And you get a side with that.

Soo-Jung: Onion rings, please.

Waitress: And for you, sir?

Chang-Su: I'd like the roast chicken, please.

Waitress: And what would you like with that?

Chang-Su: A side of coleslaw.

Waitress: All right. That's one macaroni and cheese with onion rings and one roast chicken with coleslaw.

Unit 10, Page 121, Exercise D

Waitress: Hi, welcome to Mom's Café. Are you ready to order?

Customer: Yes, I'd like a hamburger.

Waitress: And what would you like with that?

Customer: French fries, please. And a small salad.

Waitress: Can I get you anything to drink?

Customer: Do you have bottled water?

Waitress: Yes, we do.

Customer: Great. I'll have that.

Waitress: All right. That's a hamburger with a side of French fries, a small salad, and a bottled water.

Customer: That's right.

Waitress: Very good. I'll be right back with your salad.

Unit 11, Page 123, Exercise C

1. **A:** Would you like eggs for breakfast?
   B: No, I can't eat eggs. If I eat them, I have an allergic reaction.

2. **A:** My grandfather went to the hospital this morning.
   B: Oh, no. What's the matter?
   A: He had chest pains. He almost had a heart attack.

3. **A:** Be careful with that knife.
   B: Ow!
   A: Uh-oh. Your finger is bleeding. Here, let me help you.

4. **A:** Is the soup hot?
   B: Yes, very hot. Don't burn yourself. Let it cool.

5. **A:** There was an ambulance at the café.
   B: Really? What happened?
   A: A woman was choking. She had some food stuck in her throat.

Unit 11, Page 125, Exercise D

Operator: 9-1-1. What's your emergency?

Kwan: A woman fell and hit her head. She's bleeding badly.

Operator: Is she unconscious?

Kwan: No, she isn't.

Operator: OK. What's the location of the emergency?

Kwan: I'm in the Golden Apple Restaurant at 1045 North Adams Street.

Operator: What are the cross streets?

Kwan: 25th and 26th Avenues.

Operator: And what's your name?

Kwan: Kwan Park.

Operator: All right, Mr. Park. An ambulance is on its way. But don't hang up. Stay on the line with me until the ambulance gets there.

Unit 11, Page 126, Exercise A

Tina Morales: Is your home safe from fire? This is Tina Green from News 12, and I'm talking to Fire Chief Bill Adams today. Chief Adams, welcome to the program.

Bill Adams: Thank you.

Tina Morales: So, how can we make our homes safe from fire?

Bill Adams: Number one. Be careful with matches. Don't put matches where children can get them.

Tina Morales: Good point.

Bill Adams: And be careful with electrical plugs. Don't put too many electrical plugs in an electrical outlet.

Tina Morales: Electrical plugs can be dangerous.

Bill Adams: Electrical cords can be dangerous, too. Don't put an electrical cord under a rug.

Tina Morales: Any other tips?

Bill Adams: Be careful with lamps. Don't put a cloth on a lamp. It will get hot and start a fire.

Tina Morales: We need to be careful with anything hot.

Bill Adams: That's right. In winter, we have problems with heaters. Never put a heater close to a curtain.

Tina Morales: Keep heaters away from the window curtains.

Bill Adams: And one more safety rule. Make sure the windows in your house are easy to open. Don't put furniture in front of a window. If there's a fire, you want to open the window and get out.

Tina Morales: Important information, Chief. Thanks for talking with us today.

Unit 11, Page 132, Exercise B

Officer: Good afternoon. I need to see your driver's license and registration.

Driver: OK. Here they are.

Officer: Please turn off your engine and stay in your car. I'll be back in a moment.

[a few minutes later]

Officer: Sir, I pulled you over for not wearing a seat belt. I'm giving you a warning this time. Please drive safely.

Unit 12, Page 135, Exercise C

1. My name is Nina. I work in a supermarket. I make sandwiches in the deli. I clock in at 7:00 A.M. Before I start work, I wash my hands. When I prepare food, I have to wear gloves. And I have to clean the equipment often.

2. Hi. I'm Anthony. I build houses. I wear safety gear to protect my head, my eyes, and my hands. I use a lot of tools and equipment. After I finish work for the day, I have to clean my equipment. Then I store the equipment in my truck.

3. My name is Leona. I work at a hotel. I clock in at 8:00 A.M. and I work until 4:00 P.M. I clean rooms and vacuum the carpets. I have to wear a uniform. After I finish work, I store my equipment in a closet.

Unit 12, Page 137, Exercise B

Company Policies

Welcome to the Greenville Café! Below is a list of our company policies. If you have any questions, please ask your supervisor.

1. Employees must park behind the restaurant in the employee parking lot.
2. Employees must not clock in or out for other employees.
3. Employees have to wear a uniform: a white shirt and black pants.
4. Employees must take breaks at a scheduled time.
5. Employees must pass a food safety class.
6. Employees have to go to an employee meeting every month.
7. Employees have to get their schedules every Monday.
8. Employees can't be late for work more than three times.

Unit 12, Page 140, Exercise B

1. **A:** I'd like to change my hours next week. Who do I talk to about my schedule?
   B: You should talk to Walter. He's the assistant manager.
   A: OK. Thanks.
2. **A:** Karen, when do I take my break?
   B: You started today at 9:00. Take your break at 12:30.
   A: All right.
3. **A:** The new schedule is on the wall.
   B: Oh good. Which days do I have off this week?
   A: Hmm, you have Wednesday and Friday off.
4. **A:** Excuse me, where is the break room?
   B: It's the second door on the left.
   A: Thanks.

Unit 12, Page 144, Exercise B

1. **Bae:** Hi, Kristen. Could I talk to you for a minute?
   Kristen: Of course. What's up?
   Bae: Could I leave work a little early on Thursday? My son is graduating from kindergarten at 4 o'clock.
   Kristen: Well, can you stay a little later this afternoon?
   Bae: Yes, I can. No problem.

2. **Miguel:** Can you work overtime on Saturday, Angelica?
   Angelica: Well, I take my children to swim class on Saturday mornings.
   Miguel: Could you come Saturday afternoon? Janet is out sick and I need someone to cover her hours.
   Angelica: Sure. Can I come at 1:00?
   Miguel: That's great. Thanks.

Answer Key

UNIT 1

Page 2, Exercise A

Facial hair	Hair type	Hair length	Height	Weight
a beard	straight	short	average height	average weight
a goatee	curly	long	short	heavy
a mustache	wavy	shoulder-length	tall	thin

Page 2, Exercise B

1. short / straight / black
2. short / curly / brown
3. long / wavy / red
4. shoulder-length / straight / blond

A. Claudia
B. Ahmed
C. Suyin
D. Saul

Page 3, Exercise C

Michael: short hair, tall, thin, a moustache
Cha-Ram: long hair, straight hair, average weight, short
Alexandra: curly hair, shoulder-length hair, heavy, average height

Page 3, Exercise D

Answers will vary.

Page 4, Exercise A

1. have
2. is
3. are
4. isn't / doesn't have
5. doesn't have / has

Page 4, Exercise B

1. doesn't have
2. have
3. is
4. has
5. aren't
6. are
7. don't have

Page 5, Exercise C

1. True
2. False
3. False
4. False
5. False
6. True

Page 5, Exercise D

Answers will vary, but could include:

1. Andrey has short hair.
2. Ziwei is short.
3. Usain is tall.
4. Lars has long hair.
5. Guillermo is handsome.

Page 6, Exercise A

1. apartment
2. date of birth
3. female
4. height
5. weight
6. black
7. brown

Page 6, Exercise B

1. Gonzalez
2. Clearwater
3. Florida
4. 1978
5. 5 / 6
6. black
7. brown

Page 7, Exercise C

Page 7, Exercise D

Answers will vary.

Page 7, Exercise E

Answers will vary.

Page 8, Exercise A

1. and
2. and
3. but
4. and
5. but
6. and
7. but
8. but

Page 8, Exercise B

Answers will vary, but could include:

1. Oscar is friendly but he's a little shy. OR Oscar is funny and he tells great jokes.
2. Chung-Ho is out-going but she's a little bossy. OR Chung-Ho is talkative and she likes to tell stories.
3. Jason is shy and he gets nervous when he meets people. OR Jason loves to travel and visit new places.
4. Noelle is hard-working but she likes to relax after work. OR Noelle's husband says she's moody but she's laid-back.

Page 9, Exercise C

1. Jun is thin and Hwang is, too.
2. Mr. Lee isn't tall and Mr. Peters isn't, either.
3. Sally's hair isn't curly and Olivia's isn't, either.
4. Alexander is handsome and his brothers are, too.
5. The boys aren't shy and the girls aren't, either.

6. My sister is outgoing and I am, too.
7. Kevin isn't quiet and you aren't, either.

Page 9, Exercise D

Answers will vary, but could include:

1. Lydia and Viktor are tall and Kwon-Su is, too.
2. Viktor is average weight and Luz is, too.
3. Edwin is thin and Lydia is, too.
4. Luz isn't heavy and Viktor isn't, either.
5. Victor isn't funny and Kwon-Su isn't, either.
6. Edwin isn't funny and Viktor isn't either.

Page 10, Before You Read

identity theft

Page 11, Exercise A

b

Page 11, Exercise B

1. They can open a credit card account. / They can borrow money from a bank. / They can rent an apartment. / They can open a telephone account in your name.
2. Thieves look through garbage for papers such as bank statements. / Thieves steal purses and wallets. / Thieves ask for personal information by phone or e mail.

Page 11, Exercise C

1. credit card receipts / medical papers
2. address
3. social security number
4. phone / e-mail

Page 11, Exercise D

Answers will vary.

Page 12, Exercise A

1. Is Pam friendly?
2. Are Mr. and Mrs. Garcia from Mexico?

3. Are you married?
4. Where is your school?
5. How old are the students?
6. Who is your teacher?
7. When is your birthday?
8. What is your name?

Page 12, Exercise B

1. aren't   5. isn't
2. is   6. am
3. am not   7. are
4. aren't

Page 13, Exercise C

1. Where _is Ernesto from?_
2. What _is your phone number?_
3. When _is English class?_
4. How old _is your daughter?_
5. What _is your country like?_
6. Where _are you from?_

Page 13, Exercise D

Answers will vary, but could include:

1. What is your country like?
2. What do you do?
3. How old are you?
4. Do you have children?
5. Are you from Ecuador?
6. Are you married?

Page 13, Exercise E

Answers will vary.

UNIT 2

Page 14, Exercise A

Related by birth: aunt, granddaughter, nephew, niece, mother, sister

Related by marriage: brother-in-law, daughter-in-law, fiancé, mother-in-law, wife, husband

Page 14, Exercise B

1. husband and wife
2. brother-in-law and sister-in-law
3. sisters
4. mother-in-law and son-in-law
5. mother and daughter
6. brothers

7. aunt and niece
8. grandfather and grandson

Page 15, Exercise C

1. parents
2. children / son and daughter
3. brother-in-law
4. father
5. grandfather
6. brother
7. sister
8. nephew

Page 15, Exercise D

Answers will vary.

Page 16, Exercise A

1. lives / works / has
2. live / work / have
3. lives / works / has
4. live / have / work

Page 16, Exercise B

1. Alicia and Carlos don't live on Franklin Street.
2. Camille doesn't work in a hospital.
3. I don't have two jobs.
4. Deshi and Bao don't live in Florida.
5. You don't have four sisters.
6. Manuel doesn't live downtown.

Page 17, Exercise C

1. live   6. works
2. live   7. have
3. lives   8. don't have
4. work   9. don't have
5. doesn't work 10. live

Page 17, Exercise D

1. True   4. False
2. True   5. True
3. False   6. True

Page 17, Exercise E

Answers will vary.

Page 18, Exercise A

a

Page 19, Exercise B

1. d   2. b   3. a
4. e   5. c

Page 19, Exercise C

1. Housing in some areas of the U.S. is hard to find. / Living together helps family members save money. / Family members can help one another in other ways, too.
2. There isn't much privacy. / It's never quiet in a big family.

Page 19, Exercise D

Answers will vary.

Page 20, Exercise A

1. does   5. do
2. do   6. don't
3. does   7. don't
4. doesn't   8. doesn't

Page 20, Exercise B

1. Jason and I live in Miami and our sister does, too.
2. Yolanda works for a computer company and her brother-in-law does, too.
3. Our parents don't live near a park and we don't, either.
4. Edward works from 8:00 to 5:00 and his daughters do, too.
5. Henri doesn't have any sisters and I don't, either.
6. I don't work on Sunday and my husband doesn't, either.

Page 21, Exercise C

1. Phil has _red hair_ and Ben _does, too_.
2. Phil _lives_ in Las Vegas and Ben _does, too_.
3. Phil _works_ for a computer company and Ben _does, too_.
4. Phil's parents _don't_ live in Las Vegas and Ben's parents _don't, either_.
5. Phil's _parents_ live in Ohio and Ben's parents _do, too_.

Page 21, Exercise D

1. Carol _lives in_ Atlanta and Alan and Brian _do, too_.
2. Alan _has_ curly hair, and Carol _does, too_.
3. Angela _doesn't work at_ a hospital, and Carol _doesn't, either_.
4. Carol and Deborah _have_ brown hair, and Brian _does, too_.
5. Brian _doesn't have_ curly hair, and Deborah _doesn't, either_.
6. Alan _has_ a mustache, and Brian _does, too_.
7. Angela _doesn't have_ straight, brown hair, and Alan _doesn't, either_.
8. Carol _doesn't live in_ Memphis, and Brian _doesn't, either_.

Page 22, Exercise A

1. letter
2. mailing tube
3. large envelope
4. postcard
5. package

Page 22, Exercise B

Answers will vary, but could include:

1. You can send a postcard by _First-Class Mail_.
2. It takes _1–2_ days for an Express Mail letter to arrive.
3. You can send a _40_-pound package by Priority Mail.
4. You can send a 12-ounce mailing tube by _Express or Priority Mail_.
5. With _COD_, the person you send the item to pays the cost of mailing.
6. With _Insurance_, you get money back if the package is lost.

Page 23, Exercise C

1. b   2. b   3. c

Page 23, Exercise D

1. Express Mail, Priority Mail, First-Class Mail / Certified Mail
2. Express Mail, Priority Mail / Insurance

Page 23, Exercise E

Answers will vary.

Page 24, Exercise A

1. Do   4. Does
2. Does   5. Do
3. Do   6. Does

Page 24, Exercise B

1. A: Does / live
   B: he does
2. A: Do / have
   B: I don't
3. A: Does / mail
   B: she does
4. A: Does / live
   B: he does
5. A: Do / visit
   B: they don't
6. A: Do / keep
   B: we do

Page 25, Exercise C

1. Where do you live?
2. How many brothers and sisters do you have?
3. How often do you call your best friend?
4. Where do you study English?
5. When do you visit your family?
6. How do you keep in touch with your family?

Page 25, Exercise D

1. Where does Franco live?
2. When does Dorothea work?
3. How many cousins do you have?
4. How often does Jackie e-mail her family?
5. Where does your youngest daughter, Hey-Jin, live?
6. How do Mr. and Mrs. Shuh keep in touch with their son?

Page 25, Exercise E

Answers will vary.

UNIT 3

Page 26, Exercise A

1. jacket
2. boots
3. jeans
4. scarf
5. coat
6. raincoat
7. sweatshirt
8. gloves
9. windbreaker

Page 27, Exercise B

leather: sweatshirt
wool: windbreaker
fleece: raincoat
denim: boots
corduroy: scarf
vinyl: jeans

Page 27, Exercise C

Servet: a hat, a jacket, jeans
Yulan: a scarf, a coat, gloves, boots

Page 27, Exercise D

Answers will vary.

Page 28, Exercise A

1. to buy
2. to save
3. find
4. to return
5. to leave
6. to exchange
7. spend

Page 28, Exercise B

1. doesn't want to buy
2. don't need to return
3. don't need to drive
4. don't want to spend
5. don't want to go
6. doesn't want to exchange

Page 29, Exercise C

Answers will vary, but could include:

1. Charles needs to exchange a jacket.
2. Maria wants to exchange a windbreaker.
3. Tai-Ling wants to buy a dress.
4. Pietro needs to buy a sweatshirt.
5. Joe wants to buy cowboy boots.

Page 29, Exercise D

Answers will vary.

Page 30, Exercise A

1. $7.60
2. $7.58
3. $16.18
4. $5.73

Page 30, Exercise B

1. ClothesMart
2. $40
3. 09/07/10
4. $52.42
5. 15% or $3.89
6. $20.00

Page 31, Exercise C

Circle: nylon windbreaker, corduroy jacket, vinyl raincoat

Page 31, Exercise D

1. Discount 10% [should be 25%]
2. No mistakes
3. Discount 20% [should be 30%]
4. $25.00 [should be $15.00]

Page 32, Exercise A

Hi Beatriz,

I'm happy you_'re going to visit_ us this weekend! Please come on Sunday because our family _is going to be_ busy on Saturday. We_'re going to do_ some spring cleaning. Fernando _is going to do_ the laundry and I_'m going to clean_ the bathroom. Our kids, José and Manny, _are going to clean_ their rooms. In the afternoon, my mother-in-law _is going to take_ the kids to the movies. Fernando and I _are going to paint_ the living room and wash the floors. The house _is going to look_ beautiful when you see it on Sunday! See you soon!
Evelia

Page 32, Exercise B

1. Evelia isn't going to relax on Saturday. She's going to be busy.
2. Beatriz isn't going to visit on Saturday. She's going to visit on Sunday.
3. The children aren't going to clean the bathroom. They're going to clean their rooms.
4. Evelia's mother-in-law isn't going to take Fernando to a movie. She's going to take the kids to a movie.
5. Fernando and Evelia aren't going to paint the bedroom. They're going to paint the living room.
6. Fernando and Evelia aren't going to wash the floors on Sunday. They're going to wash the floors on Saturday.

Page 33, Exercise C

Irene: I can't wait for Jeff's birthday party tonight! Do I need to bring anything?
Cindy: Well, let's see. Scott _is going to get_ some ice cream on his way home from work. Alex and Nina _are going to bring_ pizza and soda. I_'m going to bake_ a cake.
Irene: Did you remember the decorations?
Cindy: Yes. My sister _is going to buy_ balloons and party games.
Irene: Cake, ice cream, pizza, games . . . sounds like it_'s going to be_ a fun party!
Cindy: Oh no! I need to go to the store.
Irene: Why?
Cindy: I forgot something very important. I forgot to buy Jeff's birthday present!

Page 33, Exercise D

1. Monique is going to clean her house.
2. Alfonso and Ana are going to hang out with friends.
3. Ji-Su is going to cook lunch for her kids.
4. James and Bernard are going to go home and relax.
5. Javier is going to get lunch at a deli.

Page 34, Exercise A

b

Page 35, Exercise B

1. 1
2. 3
3. 4
4. 5
5. 2

Page 35, Exercise C

Answers will vary.

Page 36, Exercise A

1. too
2. very
3. too
4. very / too

Page 36, Exercise B

1. too
2. very
3. very
4. too
5. very
6. very / too

Page 36, Exercise C

1. b   2. a   3. b   4. a   5. b

Page 37, Exercise D

Matt:
The hat is too small.
The pants are too long.
The seam is split.
The shoes are too big.

Jake:
The hat is too big.
The pants are too big.
The jacket is too small.
The shoes are too big.

UNIT 4

Page 38, Exercise A

1. go fishing
2. go swimming
3. go out to eat
4. go hiking
5. go dancing
6. go shopping
7. go for a bike ride
8. go for a walk

Page 38, Exercise B

go: dancing, fishing, jogging
go to the: beach, zoo, park
go for a: bike ride, walk

Page 39, Exercise C

Answers will vary, but could include:

My family is very active. We like to spend our free time outdoors. Some weekends, we go to the park. My wife and I like to _go for a walk_ and our children _ride their bikes_. Some weekends, we _go hiking_ in the mountains. The view from the top is beautiful! We also like to _go to the beach_. We all love being near the water. My wife and kids love to _swim_, and I like to _go fishing_. The only problem is that I never catch any fish!

Page 39, Exercise D

Answers will vary.

Page 40, Exercise A

1. always / never
2. hardly ever
3. usually
4. sometimes
5. sometimes

Page 40, Exercise B

1. We usually go fishing on Sundays.
2. Benita always goes dancing on Saturday nights.
3. My wife and I never go out to eat.
4. Ben and Janice go hiking often in the summer. / Ben and Janice often go hiking in the summer.
5. My father hardly ever goes shopping.

Page 41, Exercise C

1. How often do the children go swimming?
2. How often does the family go for a bike ride?
3. How often does Dolores work late?
4. How often do Alfredo and Dolores go out to eat?
5. How often does the family visit Grandma?

Page 41, Exercise D

Answers will vary, but could include:

1. The children go swimming once a month.
2. The family goes for a bike ride once a week.
3. Dolores works late twice a month.
4. Alfredo and Dolores go out to eat once a month.
5. The family visits Grandma twice a month.

Page 42, Exercise A

1. The ESL class meets on _Tuesdays and Thursdays_ from _9:00_ A.M. to _12:00_ P.M.
2. The cooking class meets every _Monday_ at _6:30_ P.M.
3. The Dance Club meets on the first and third _Saturday_ of the month from _8:00_ to _10:00_ P.M.
4. The painting class starts at _11:00_ A.M. and ends at _1:00_ P.M.

Page 42, Exercise B

1. The Bike Club meets on the first Sunday of the month from 8:00 to 11:00 A.M.
2. The Movie Club meets on the second and fourth Saturday of the month from 8:00 to 10:00 P.M.
3. The computer class starts at 1:00 P.M.

Page 43, Exercise C

1. b   2. a   3. a   4. a   5. a

Page 43, Exercise D

Sunday	Monday	Tuesday	Wednesday	Thursday	Friday	Saturday
		1 English class 5:30 to 7:00 P.M.	2 Swimming class 4:00 to 6:00 P.M.	3 English class 5:30 to 7:00 P.M.	4	5 Movie Night 7:30 P.M.
6 The Walking Club 7:00 to 8:00 A.M	7 Dance class 7:00 to 9:00 P.M.	8 English class 5:30 to 7:00 P.M. Columbus Day	9 Swimming class 4:00 to 6:00 P.M.	10 English class 5:30 to 7:00 P.M.	11	12 Movie Night 7:30 P.M.
13 The Walking Club 7:00 to 8:00 A.M.	14	15 English class 5:30 to 7:00 P.M.	16 Swimming class 4:00 to 6:00 P.M.	17 English class 5:30 to 7:00 P.M.	18	19 Movie Night 7:30 P.M.
20 The Walking Club 7:00 to 8:00 A.M.	21 Dance class 7:00 to 9:00 P.M.	22 English class 5:30 to 7:00 P.M.	23 Swimming class 4:00 to 6:00 P.M.	24 English class 5:30 to 7:00 P.M.	25	26 Movie Night 7:30 P.M.
27 The Walking Club 7:00 to 8:00 A.M.	28	29 English class 5:30 to 7:00 P.M.	30 Swimming class 4:00 to 6:00 P.M.	31 English class 5:30 to 7:00 P.M. Halloween		

Page 44, Exercise A

1. like to take
2. don't like to study
3. hates to iron
4. like to go
5. doesn't like to stay home
6. likes to go
7. hates to get up
8. doesn't like to swim

Page 44, Exercise B

1. likes to
2. like to
3. love to
4. don't like to
5. doesn't like to
6. doesn't like to
7. hates to
8. loves to

Page 45, Exercise C

1.

	Rick	Angie
go hiking	✓	
go to the beach		✓

2.

	Fred	Liz
eat Italian food	✓	✓
go dancing		✓

Page 45, Exercise D

Answers will vary, but could include:

1. Mathew loves to go fishing.
2. Mathew hates to get up early.
3. Mathew loves to do karate.
4. Mathew hates to go shopping.
5. Mathew loves to walk his dog.
6. Mathew hates to cook.

Page 46, Exercise A

c

Page 47, Exercise B

1. 15
2. small, inexpensive gift
3. expensive gift
4. pass it to you
5. please eat

Page 47, Exercise C

1. Rude
2. Polite
3. Rude
4. Polite
5. Polite

Page 47, Exercise D

Answers will vary.

Page 48, Exercise A

1. to cook
2. to meet
3. to exercise
4. to take
5. to pay
6. to get up

Page 48, Exercise B

Chuck: Guess what? I got free tickets to the zoo. Do you and the kids want to go this Saturday?

Melinda: That sounds like fun, but I _have to work_ this Saturday

Chuck: Oh. Do you have any plans on Sunday?

Melinda: Well, I don't, but Barry _has to go_ to his guitar class. And Tina _has to play_ in a soccer game. How about next Saturday? I _don't have to work_ that day.

Chuck: Hmm. Actually, I _have to take_ my mother to a wedding. Can you go on Sunday?

Melinda: No, Sunday's not good. I _have to help_ my sister. She's moving to a new apartment.

Chuck: Oh, well. Too bad.

Page 49, Exercise C

Answers will vary, but could include:

1. Sorry, I can't. I have to go to my computer class.
2. Yes, I do.
3. Sorry, I can't. I have to go to my ESL class.
4. Sorry, I can't. I have to go to Miguel's birthday party.
5. Sorry, I can't. I have to have lunch with my mom and dad.

UNIT 5

Page 50, Exercise A

1. c 2. d 3. e 4. b 5. a

Page 50, Exercise B

1. stuck
2. no heat
3. leaking
4. no hot water
5. working

Page 51, Exercise C

1. The door is stuck.
2. There's no heat.
3. The ceiling is leaking.
4. The toilet is clogged.
5. There's no hot water.
6. The washing machine isn't working.

Page 51, Exercise D

Answers will vary.

Page 52, Exercise A

1. is
2. am
3. are
4. is
5. are
6. are
7. is

Page 52, Exercise B

1. is painting
2. is talking
3. isn't calling
4. 'm e-mailing
5. is looking
6. isn't fixing
7. 's buying
8. isn't working
9. is using

Page 53, Exercise C

Answers will vary but could include:

1. The dishwasher is leaking in apartment 3.
2. Two people are painting in apartment 4.
3. A woman is fixing the lock in the entrance.
4. The toilet is clogged in apartment 6.
5. The oven is broken in apartment 5.
6. The man in apartment 2 is calling the building manager.

Page 54, Exercise A

1. Furnished
2. Bedroom
3. Bathroom
4. Apartment
5. Floor
6. Living room
7. Dining room
8. Eat-in kitchen
9. Heat
10. Hot water
11. Included
12. Washer / Dryer
13. Basement
14. Air-conditioning
15. Near
16. Transportation
17. Month
18. Security deposit

Page 54, Exercise B

Answers will vary, but could include:

1. The apartment has two bedrooms.
2. The apartment is furnished.
3. The apartment has a small eat-in kitchen.
4. Hot water is not included in the rent.
5. There is air-conditioning.
6. The apartment is near shopping.
7. The security deposit is half of one month's rent.

Page 55, Exercise C

1. B
2. A
3. B
4. A
5. B
6. B
7. A
8. B

Page 55, Exercise D

Answers will vary.

Page 56, Exercise A

Jackie: Hello?
Charlie: Hi, Jackie. This is Charlie at Richmond Realty. I have a nice _apartment_ to show you.
Jackie: Great! Tell me about it.
Charlie: Well, it's really nice. There are three _bedrooms_. And there's a large _living room_.
Jackie: How many _bathrooms_ are there?
Charlie: Two.
Jackie: Is there a dining room?
Charlie: There's no dining room, but there's a big _eat-in kitchen_.
Jackie: Sounds good. How's the location? Is there a _park_ nearby?
Charlie: Yes, there is. Right around the corner.
Jackie: And is the neighborhood quiet?
Charlie: Yes, it's on a very quiet street. There isn't a lot of _traffic_.
Jackie: Wow. That sounds perfect. Can I see it today?

Page 56, Exercise B

1. There _are_ no pets allowed in the building.
2. _Is_ there a supermarket nearby?
3. How many bathrooms _are_ there?
4. There isn't a bus stop near here. / There _is_ no bus stop near here.
5. _Are_ there a lot of stores in the neighborhood?
6. There _are_ three bedrooms.

Page 57, Exercise C

Answers will vary, but could include:

1. Is there air-conditioning?
2. Is parking included?
3. Are there shops nearby?
4. Is it near a bus stop?
5. How many bedrooms are there?
6. Is there a laundry room?
7. Is there a lot of traffic on the street?
8. Is there a park nearby?

Page 57, Exercise D

Answers will vary, but could include:

1. There is no air-conditioning.
2. There is no parking.
3. There are no shops nearby.
4. There are no parks in the area.
5. It's near a bus stop.
6. It has three bedrooms.
7. It has a laundry room in the basement.
8. There is no traffic on the street.

Page 58, Exercise A

c

Page 59, Exercise B

1. security deposit
2. certified letter
3. stove
4. paying her rent
5. court

Page 59, Exercise C

Answers will vary, but could include:

1. Viet wants to know if the landlord can keep his security deposit.
2. The landlord can keep the deposit, but he needs to send a certified letter explaining the problems.
3. Alejandra wants to know if she can stop paying the rent because the stove is broken.
4. Alejandra can stop paying the rent, but the landlord can take her to court.

Page 59, Exercise D

Answers will vary.

Page 60, Exercise A

1. supermarket
2. high school
3. pharmacy
4. hotel
5. park
6. hospital

Page 61, Exercise B

1. c   2. a   3. b   4. b   5. a

Page 61, Exercise C

Directions to the hospital:
Go straight on Miller Street.
__Go through__ two traffic lights.
Turn ___left___ onto Ventura Avenue.
Go through three ___stop signs___.
The hospital is on the ___right___.

UNIT 6

Page 62, Exercise A

1. an anniversary party
2. a surprise party
3. a graduation party
4. a funeral
5. a potluck party
6. a birthday party
7. a family reunion
8. a wedding
9. a retirement party

Page 63, Exercise B

1. a wedding
2. a retirement party
3. a potluck party
4. an anniversary party
5. a family reunion
6. a surprise party
7. a funeral
8. a graduation party

Page 63, Exercise C

1. a potluck party
2. a retirement party
3. a surprise party
4. a family reunion

Page 64, Exercise A

Amy and Tom _stayed_ at home yesterday. Amy _baked_ cookies and Tom _cleaned_ the kitchen. They both _washed_ the dishes. Tom _fixed_ a leaking faucet and Amy _painted_ the front door. They _worked_ hard. In the evening, Amy and Tom _wanted_ to relax, so they _went_ to an Italian restaurant for dinner.

Page 64, Exercise B

Rich: How was the _family reunion_?
Ann: Very nice. We all missed you.
Rich: Yeah. I was sorry I couldn't go. Who was there?
Ann: The whole family _showed_ up. All the aunts, uncles, and cousins.
Rich: Aunt Lucy, too?
Ann: Of course. Everyone listened to her _family stories_. And we looked at old photos and _watched movies_ of Grandma and Grandpa's wedding.
Rich: Oh yeah? I'm sorry I missed that!
Ann: Well, you should have come! We had a great time. We _stayed up late_ and _talked all night_.
Rich: Really? I'll definitely have to go next time!

Page 65, Exercise C

Answers will vary, but could include:

1. In-Ho and Sun-Ah danced at the barbecue.
2. John cooked hamburgers at the barbecue.
3. Hannah and James talked at the barbecue.
4. David played his guitar at the barbecue.
5. Min-Je and Jae-in played soccer at the barbecue.
6. Judy sang at the barbecue.

Page 65, Exercise D

Answers will vary.

Page 66, Exercise A

1. Independence Day
2. Memorial Day
3. Martin Luther King Jr. Day
4. New Year's Day
5. Labor Day
6. Columbus Day
7. Presidents' Day
8. Veterans' Day
9. Thanksgiving Day
10. Christmas Day

Page 67, Exercise B

Jan. 1: New Year's Day, Jan. 18: Martin Luther King Jr. Day, Feb. 15: Presidents' Day, May 31: Memorial Day, Jul. 4: Independence Day, Sept. 6: Labor Day, Oct. 13: Columbus Day, Nov. 11: Veterans' Day, Nov. 25: Thanksgiving Day, Dec. 25: Christmas Day

Page 67, Exercise C

Answers will vary.

Page 68, Exercise A

1. went
2. didn't get
3. came
4. made
5. grew
6. didn't take
7. got married

Page 68, Exercise B

1. Diana didn't leave home at age 18.
2. Jun didn't get a job in a cafeteria.
3. I didn't have a big wedding when I got married.
4. Marcos didn't go to a community college to study business.
5. Estelle didn't begin her new job yesterday.
6. My mother didn't make my wedding dress.

Page 69, Exercise C

1. A: *Did you have a big wedding?*
   B: No, *I didn't*. I had a small wedding.
2. A: *Did you graduate last year?*
   B: Yes, *I did.* I graduated last December.
3. A: *Did Javad get a job at a bank?*
   B: No, *he didn't*. He got a job at a school.
4. A: *Did Lin meet her husband in 2002?*
   B: Yes, *she did*. They met in January, 2002.
5. A: *Did Laila always want to be a teacher?*
   B: No, *she didn't*. She wanted to be a nurse.
6. A: *Did you grow up in a small city?*
   B: No, *I didn't*. I grew up in a big city.

Page 69, Exercise D

1. Was your son born in the U.S.?
2. Did Santos grow up in California?
3. Did your brothers move to the United States?
4. Were you born in Russia?
5. Did Magda take English classes last month?

Page 70, Before You Read

Howard Schultz is the president of Starbucks. Howard got a job at Starbucks in 1982.

Page 71, Exercise A

1. False
   Howard's family lived in a poor neighborhood in New York.
2. True
3. False
   Howard graduated from college.
4. False
   In 1982, Starbucks sold coffee drinks but no sandwiches.
5. True
6. True
7. False
   There are 15,000 Starbucks coffee shops in 43 countries.
8. True

Page 71, Exercise B

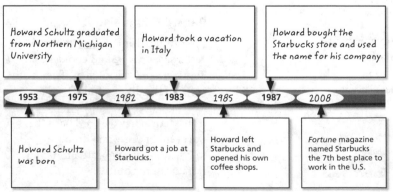

Page 72, Exercise A

1. Why did you oversleep?
2. When did you have car trouble?
3. Where did you find your wallet?
4. What did you do last weekend?
5. Why did you take the wrong bus?
6. What time did you leave work last night?

Page 72, Exercise B

1. Jason overslept because he stayed up late to watch a movie on TV.
2. Jason forgot his wallet on his way to work.
3. Jason took the number 33 bus.
4. Jason got to work at 9:45.
5. Jason tried to buy his lunch at the candy machine.

Page 73, Exercise C

Answers will vary, but could include:

1. The Carlson family got stuck in traffic.
2. The Carlson family took the wrong exit.
3. The Carlson family forgot their picnic lunch food.
4. The Carlson family lost their car keys.
5. The Carlson family car broke down on the side of a highway.
6. The Carlson family was unhappy when they got stuck in traffic.

Page 73, Exercise

Answers will vary.

UNIT 7

Page 74, Exercise A

1. A   4. E   7. F
2. D   5. C   8. I
3. G   6. H   9. B

Page 75, Exercise B

1. a   6. a
2. the   7. (no word)
3. an   8. a
4. (no word)   9. a
5. (no word)   10. a

Page 75, Exercise C

Dear Grandma,

We are on vacation this week. Last weekend, we went camping at a state park. We did NOT have a good time. Dad cooked on the campfire every night. The food was really bad. Dad had ___heartburn___, and I had _an upset stomach_. On Saturday, it rained all day. Mom got sick. She had _a sore throat_ and ___a cough___. On Sunday, Janet and I went swimming. Janet got water in her ear. Now she has ___an earache___. Then Dad and I went hiking. Now I have ___a rash___ on my arms and legs. This morning we went to a hotel. No more camping for us!

Love,
Marie

Page 76, Exercise A

1. on   6. from
2. at   7. to
3. in   8. in
4. on   9. by
5. at

Page 76, Exercise B

1. on   5. at
2. in   6. by
3. from   7. in
4. to   8. on

Page 77, Exercise C

1. The appointment is on Thursday.
2. The appointment is on November 19.
3. The doctor's name is Dr. Bernard.
4. The phone number of the clinic is (313) 555-1234.
5. The clinic is on Central Street.
6. The clinic opens at 7 A.M. on Mondays.
7. The clinic closes at 7 P.M. on Saturdays.
8. The patient's appointment is in 25 minutes.
9. He should arrive at 3:25 P.M.

Page 78, Exercise A

1. patient
2. expiration date
3. over-the-counter (OTC) medicine
4. prescription
5. dosage
6. refill
7. warning

Page 78, Exercise B

1. False   4. True
2. True   5. False
3. False

Page 79, Exercise C

1. Sarah Carlton
2. Eyes
3. Four drops
4. Every 4 to 6 hours
5. No refills
6. 3/25/2013

Page 79, Exercise D

Pharmacist: Mr. Bronson, your prescription is ready. Is this the first time you are taking Naproxen?

Mr. Bronson: Yes, it is. How much do I take?

Pharmacist: Take _two_ tablets _three_ times a day.

Mr. Bronson: Do I take them with _food_?

Pharmacist: Yes. Take the tablets at breakfast, lunch, and dinner.

Mr. Bronson: And how long do I take them?

Pharmacist: _Ten days_.

Mr. Bronson: All right.

Pharmacist: This medicine can make you feel _dizzy_ or nauseous. If this happens, stop taking the medicine and call your _doctor_.

Mr. Bronson: OK.

Pharmacist: Do you understand these _directions_?

Mr. Bronson: Yes, I do. Thank you.

Page 80, Exercise A

1. got
2. cut
3. had / hurt
4. broke
5. fell / sprained

Page 80, Exercise B

1. Maria _had_ a bad accident in her house. She _fell_ down the stairs, and she _sprained_ her arm.
2. Andrew _got_ hurt at work. He _broke_ his ankle, and he _went_ to the emergency room.
3. Mei-Lin _got_ sick last week. She _had_ the flu. I _took_ her to the doctor.

Page 81, Exercise C

1. He hurt his back.
2. She broke her leg.
3. He cut his foot.
4. She fell.
5. He burned his finger.
6. She sprained her wrist.

Page 81, Exercise D

Answers will vary.

Page 82, Before You Read

hot and cold temperatures /
massage / food / aroma

Page 83, Exercise A

b

Page 83, Exercise B

1. g	4. h	7. i
2. e	5. d	8. a
3. f	6. b	9. c

Page 83, Exercise C

Answers will vary.

Page 84, Exercise A

1. because	4. because
2. for	5. for
3. for	6. because

Page 84, Exercise B

1. My daughter Ju-Yeon didn't go to
   school today _because_ she didn't
   feel well. I went to the drugstore
   for some flu medicine.
2. Eva took her baby to the clinic
   because she needed a checkup.
   The doctor asked her to come back
   next week _for_ a blood test.
3. I went to the dental clinic _because_
   I had a bad toothache. I had to
   wait a long time _because_ they
   were very busy.
4. I went to the doctor _for_ a flu shot.
   I wanted to get the shot _because_ I
   had the flu last year and I missed a
   lot of work.
5. Camila always misses class. Last
   week she was absent _because_
   she had a sore throat. Today she's
   absent _because_ she has to work.

Page 85, Exercise C

Answers will vary, but could include:

1. He went to the drugstore because
   he needed eye drops. / He went to
   the drugstore for a bottle of eye
   drops.

2. She missed work because she had a
   dentist's appointment.
3. He called 911 because he had chest
   pain.
4. She went to the doctor because she
   needed a flu shot. / She went to the
   doctor for a flu shot.
5. He called his supervisor because he
   had a cold.

UNIT 8

Page 86, Exercise A

1. d	2. b	3. a
4. c	5. e	6. f

Page 86, Exercise B

1. prepare food
2. unload materials
3. install computer hardware
4. record patient information
5. stock shelves
6. supervise employees

Page 87, Exercise C

Answers will vary, but could include:

1. Job title: food service worker
   Job duties: prepare food, clean
   kitchen equipment
2. Job title: hospital nurse
   Job duties: record patient
   information, look after patients
3. Job title: warehouse worker
   Job duties: unload materials,
   operate a forklift
4. Job title: store clerk
   Job duties: stock shelves, keep store
   organized

Page 87, Exercise D

Answers will vary.

Page 88, Exercise A

1. can type
2. can't operate
3. can't speak
4. can't use
5. can prepare
6. can order
7. can't lift

Page 88, Exercise B

1. Can you lift heavy boxes?
2. Can Ms. Navarro speak English
   well?
3. Can Diego order more spaghetti
   for the kitchen?
4. Can you type?
5. Can David work on Sundays?

Page 89, Exercise C

Answers will vary, but could include:

Stock clerk: Can you lift heavy boxes? /
Can you order supplies? / Can you
operate a forklift?

Cashier: Can you use a cash register? /
Can you speak Spanish? / Can you
assist customers?

Food service worker: Can you prepare
food? / Can you work weekends? / Do
you have experience?

Page 89, Exercise D

Answers will vary, but could include:

I'm going to give Ignacio the stock clerk
job because he can lift boxes, stock
shelves, operate a forklift, and order
supplies.

I'm going to give Marie the cashier job
because she can use a cash register.

I'm going to give Chan the food
service worker job because he can
order supplies, prepare food, and clean
kitchen equipment.

Page 90, Exercise A

1. Part-time cashier position
   available. Monday–Friday,
   evenings. Experience required.
2. Full-time bus drivers needed.
   Mornings and afternoons, $11.50
   per hour, benefits, driver's license
   required. Telephone number
   (312) 555-1234
3. Stock clerk position available, full-
   time, Monday–Friday and some
   weekends. No experience required.
   Apply in person. Bring references.

4. Nurse assistants wanted. Full-time, flexible hours. Excellent benefits. Two years of experience required. E-mail résumé to jobs@allnurses.com. Include references.

Page 90, Exercise B

1. PT receptionist pos. avail. at busy car sales office. Sat–Sun 8:00–4:00. Incl. handling phone calls and greeting customers. No exp. req. Will train right person. Tel. Gary's Classic Cars (312) 555-1234.
2. FT warehouse assistant wanted in large company. M–F 7:00–4:00. Must be able to lift up to 50 lbs. Exp. req. in operating a forklift. Excel. pay, incl. bnfts. and vacation.

Page 91, Exercise C

1. False   5. True
2. True   6. True
3. False   7. True
4. False   8. False

Page 91, Exercise D

Answers will vary, but could include:

The best match for Gilbert Reyes is the Office Assistant position because he can work full-time in an office, get health benefits, and use a computer.

Page 92, Exercise A

1. in   4. In
2. later   5. Since
3. in   6. ago

Page 92, Exercise B

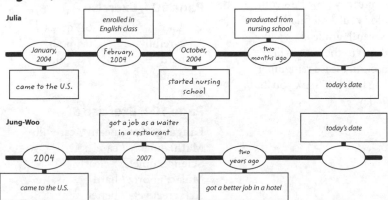

Page 93, Exercise C

Answers will vary, but could include:

Arnold Schwarzenegger was born in 1947 in Austria. In 1967, he won the Mr. Universe body-building title. One year later, he moved to the U.S. In 1970, he starred in his first movie: *Hercules in New York*. He starred in the hit movie, *The Terminator*, twelve years later. The next year, he became a U.S. citizen. He married TV news star Maria Shriver in 1986. Six years ago, in 2003, he became the governor of California.

Page 93, Exercise D

Answers will vary.

Page 94, Before You Read

Answers will vary, but could include:

Advice on how to have a successful interview

Page 95, Exercise A

a

Page 95, Exercise B

Answers will vary, but could include:

Mistakes: Dominique wore too much jewelry. Dominique wore too much perfume. Dominique did not arrive fifteen minutes early.

Correct: Dominique gave the manager a firm handshake and made eye contact. Dominique was honest about being fired from her last job.

Page 95, Exercise C

Answers will vary.

Page 96, Exercise A

1. and   4. or
2. or   5. or
3. and

Page 96, Exercise B

1.
> When can you work? Check the boxes.
> ☑ Saturday ☑ Sunday

2.
> When can you work? Check the boxes.
> ☑ first shift ☐ second shift

3.
> When can you work? Check the boxes.
> ☐ breakfast shift ☑ lunch shift
> ☐ dinner shift

4.
> When can you work? Check the boxes.
> ☑ weekdays ☐ weekends
> ☑ days ☑ evenings

Page 97, Exercise C

Coffee Stop Cafe	Employee Schedule		April 7 – April 12			
	Mon.	Tue.	Wed.	Thu.	Fri.	Sat.
Morning Shift 6:30–11:30 A.M.	Paul	Rosa	Paul	Rosa	Paul	Paul
Afternoon Shift 11:00 A.M.–4:00 P.M.	Rosa	Fang	Fang	Fang	Rosa	Fang

Page 97, Exercise D

Answers will vary.

UNIT 9

Page 98, Exercise A

1. P.E. (physical education)
2. community service
3. language arts / English
4. science
5. art
6. technology
7. social studies / history
8. math
9. music

Page 99, Exercise B

1. art
2. social studies / history
3. math
4. science

Page 99, Exercise C

1. music
2. P.E. (physical education)
3. community service
4. language arts / English
5. technology

Page 100, Exercise A

1. A: won't have
   B: will watch
2. A: will be
   B: will plan
3. A: will be
   B: won't be
4. A: will play
   B: will try

Page 100, Exercise B

1. will have
2. will visit
3. will have
4. will sing
5. will play
6. will show
7. will go
8. will give
9. will be

Page 101, Exercise C

Good morning, students. We have a busy week at Greenville Middle School. The Music Club will have a bake sale today. Club members will sell cookies and other baked goods from 11:30 to 12:30 in the cafeteria. The Technology Club will meet in the library today at 4:00. Bad news, Greenville basketball fans. There won't be a basketball game on Wednesday. The Greenville Tigers will play their next home game on Monday, at 7:00 P.M. Don't forget there will be a Back-to-school Night for parents on Thursday at 7:30. Your parents will visit your classroom and meet your teachers . . . but they won't do your homework for you! And finally, on Friday the seventh grade class will take a field trip to the Greenville Science Museum. Please remember to bring a bag lunch. Thank you and have a good day.

Page 101, Exercise D

1. The 9th grade class will collect cans of food for "Food for All" organization.
2. The 10th grade will read stories to children at the Greenville Children's Hospital.
3. The 11th Grade will paint benches and playground equipment at Silver Beach.
4. The 12th grade will clean up garbage and plant flowers at Greenville Park.

Page 102, Exercise A

1. a   2. b   3. a   4. a   5. b

Page 103, Exercise B

1. a   2. b   3. a   4. b   5. b

Page 103, Exercise C

2

Page 103, Exercise D

Date _____ Time _____
To Mrs. Miller _____

While You Were Out

From Maria Rodriguez _____
Phone (718) 555-4567 _____
Message: I have a question about Juan's science fair project

Page 104, Exercise A

1. good
2. carefully
3. hard
4. neatly
5. quickly
6. poor
7. quiet

Page 104, Exercise B

Language Arts: neatly / carefully
Math: quickly / carelessly
Science: quietly / clearly
Music: poorly / hard
Art: creatively / better

Page 105, Exercise C

1. her
2. you
3. it
4. them
5. me

Page 105, Exercise D

1. them
2. it
3. him
4. us
5. her
6. it
7. them
8. it
9. you

Page 106, Before You Read

The girl is doing homework.

Page 107, Exercise A

b

Page 107, Exercise B

Answers will vary, but could include:

BAD: The son is studying in front of the TV. The parents are not showing interest in their son. The son is not in a study area.

GOOD: The daughter is in her study area. The mom is showing interest in her daughter. The family has a homework schedule.

Page 107, Exercise C

Answers will vary.

Page 108, Exercise A

1. daughter's
2. children's
3. Ms. Wilson's
4. son's
5. parents'
6. school's
7. nephew's

Page 108, Exercise B

1. sons'
2. Mary's
3. players'
4. student's
5. principal's
6. Bill's

Page 109, Exercise C

students
children's
kids
kids'
daughters
students'
students
school's
classmates
Students
person's

Page 109, Exercise D

Answers will vary.

UNIT 10

Page 110, Exercise A

1. box
2. half-gallon
3. bag
4. can
5. bunch
6. gallon

Page 110, Exercise B

1. c
2. a
3. a
4. a
5. b
6. a

Page 111, Exercise B

1. b
2. d
3. e
4. a
5. c
6. f
7. g
8. h

Page 111, Exercise D

Answers will vary.

Page 112, Exercise A

Count nouns:

apples
grapes
olives
onions
oranges

Non-count nouns:

fish
milk
soda
sugar
yogurt

Page 112, Exercise B

1. A: _Is there any_ bread?
   B: _Yes, there's some on the counter_.
2. A: _Is there any_ fish?
   B: _Yes, there's some in the refrigerator_.
3. A: _Are there any_ apples?
   B: _Yes, there are three in the fruit bowl_.
4. A: _Are there any_ carrots?
   B: _No, there aren't any carrots_.
5. A: _Is there any_ yogurt?
   B: _Yes, there's some in the refrigerator_.
6. A: _Are there any_ bananas?
   B: _No, there aren't any bananas_.
7. A: _Is there any_ cheese?
   B: _Yes, there's some cheese in the refrigerator_.
8. A: _Is there any_ cereal?
   B: _Yes, there's some in the cabinet_.

Page 113, Exercise C

1. How many
2. How many
3. How much
4. How much
5. How many

Page 113, Exercise D

Paulo: I'm going to the supermarket. Do we need anything for dinner?

Clara: Well. I think I'm going to make some soup. Could you get some <u>chicken</u>?

Paulo: Sure. <u>How much chicken</u> do you need?

Clara: Let me check the recipe. I need <u>a pound of chicken</u>.

Paulo: OK. <u>Anything else</u>?

Clara: Let's see. <u>Are there any</u> carrots?

Paulo: Yes, there's <u>a bunch of</u> carrots in the refrigerator.

Clara: That's enough. <u>Is there any</u> olive oil?

Paulo: Yes, there's <u>a bottle of</u> olive oil in the cabinet.

Clara: Good. <u>Are there any</u> potatoes?

Paulo: Um. No, there aren't any. I'll get <u>a pound of potatoes</u>.

Page 114, Exercise A

1. c
2. f
3. b
4. e
5. a
6. d

Page 114, Exercise B

1. c
2. d
3. a

Page 115, Exercise C

1. whole grain oats
2. 190mg
3. 3g
4. 3g
5. 16g
6. 25g
7. 0mg
8. 10

Page 115, Exercise D

Answers will vary, but could include:

Toasted Oats brand cereal is better for your health. It has fewer calories and less sugar. It also has more protein and fiber. The main ingredient in Fruit Rings is sugar.

Page 116, Exercise A

1. cheaper than
2. healthier than
3. saltier than
4. more expensive / more fattening
5. more delicious

Page 116, Exercise B

Answers will vary, but could include:

1. Canned soup is easier to make than homemade soup.
2. Canned soup has more salt than homemade soup.
3. Pizza at The Italian Café is fresher than frozen pizza.
4. Frozen pizza is cheaper than pizza at The Italian Café.
5. Barbecued chicken is tastier than sandwiches.
6. Sandwiches are easier to make than barbecued chicken.

Page 117, Exercise C

Answers will vary, but could include:

1. I'll buy frozen peas. They're more convenient than fresh peas.
2. I'll buy California pears. They're fresher than canned pears.
3. I'll buy Florida oranges. Homemade juice is tastier than boxed juice.
4. I'll buy fresh Salmon fillet. It's cheaper than rib-eye steak.

Page 117, Exercise D

Answers will vary.

Page 118, Exercise A

a

Page 119, Exercise B

Answers will vary, but could include:

1. When a store pays twice the value of any coupons you bring in
2. A plan for how to save money
3. A popular and well-known product
4. Place where local farmers sell their products
5. Food that is not healthy because it contains a lot of oil or sugar

Page 119, Exercise D

1. Mayra looks in the newspaper for coupons. Mayra can save up to $20.
2. Linda and Tom take a shopping list to the supermarket. They take it so they can stay on their budget.
3. Alberto buys store-brands at the supermarket. He buys them because they are cheaper than name-brand products.
4. Jan and Chris shop at the farmer's market. They shop there because everything is fresh and cheap.
5. Jiao eats before she goes to the supermarket. She does that so that she doesn't buy too much food.

Page 119, Exercise E

Answers will vary.

Page 120, Exercise A

a few, any, any, some, some, any, a little, Some

Page 120, Exercise B

1. a 2. a 3. a 4. b 5. a

Page 121, Exercise C

a

Page 121, Exercise D

```
  ─ ─ ─ ─ ─ ─ ─ ─ ─ ─
   Guest Check

  TABLE    SERVER      CHECK #
                        04421
 ─────────────────────────────
 1 │ hamburger
   │ with French fries
 1 │ small salad
 1 │ bottled water
```

Page 121, Exercise E

Answers will vary.

UNIT 11

Page 122, Exercise A

1. He's choking.
2. She burned herself.
3. He swallowed poison.
4. She's bleeding.
5. He fell.
6. She's having trouble breathing.
7. She's unconscious.
8. He's having a heart attack.
9. He's having an allergic reaction.

Page 123, Exercise B

1. c   2. a   3. d   4. b   5. e

Page 123, Exercise C

1. an allergic reaction
2. a heart attack
3. bleeding
4. burn yourself
5. choking

Page 123, Exercise D

Answers will vary.

Page 124, Exercise A

1. A: Why _is_ this little boy _crying_?
   B: His elbow _is bleeding_.

2. A: _Are_ you _feeling_ OK? You don't look well.
   B: I don't know what's wrong. I'_m having_ trouble breathing.
3. A: What'_s happening_ downtown?
   B: I'm not sure. There are a lot of fire trucks in the street.
4. A: _Are_ the fire trucks _coming_?
   B: Yes, don't worry. I hear them now.
5. A: Why _is_ he _taking_ his son to the emergency room?
   B: His son ate some peanuts, and he'_s having_ an allergic reaction.

Page 124, Exercise B

A: 9-1-1. What's your emergency?
B: It's my neighbor. She'_s having_ trouble breathing.
A: OK. Tell me what'_s happening_. Are you with your neighbor now?
B: Yes, she'_s lying_ on the floor of my apartment.
A: Is she unconscious?
B: No, she's awake. My daughters _are talking_ to her.
A: What's your location?
B: 180 Fifth Street. I'_m calling_ from apartment 12 on the second floor.

Page 125, Exercise C

1. What's the emergency?
2. Is the woman bleeding?
3. Is the woman unconscious?
4. What's the location of the emergency?
5. What are the cross streets?
6. Who is calling 911?
7. What is happening now?

Page 125, Exercise D

1. A woman fell and hit her head.
2. Yes, she's bleeding badly.
3. No, she isn't.
4. The Golden Apple Restaurant at 1045 North Adams Street
5. 25th and 26th Avenues.
6. Kwan Park
7. An ambulance is on its way.

Page 125, Exercise E

Answers will vary.

Page 126, Exercise A

1. matches
2. plugs / outlet
3. rug
4. cloth
5. curtain
6. in front of

Page 126, Exercise B

1. smoke alarm
2. exits
3. fire extinguisher
4. fire escape
5. escape plan

Page 127, Exercise C

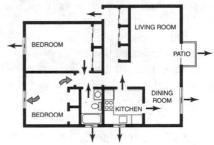

Page 127, Exercise D

Answers will vary.

Page 128, Exercise A

1. a robbery
2. an explosion
3. a car accident
4. a construction accident

Page 128, Exercise B

There was
There were
There were
there weren't
There was
There were
There was
There wasn't
There was

Page 129, Exercise C

Answers will vary, but could include:

1. There was a car accident on Seventh Avenue.
2. There were many injuries.
3. There was a fire truck.
4. There was a gas truck explosion.
5. There were crowds of people.
6. There was a traffic jam.

Page 130, Exercise A

c

Page 131, Exercise B

Answers will vary, but could include:

1. There was an accident. A car drove into Lake Jordan.
2. Jamie Torres called 911. The passengers in the car were hurt.
3. Miguel Torres smashed the car window with a pipe.
4. Miguel rescued the boy first.
5. Miguel rescued the woman next.
6. When the police officer arrived, the car was underwater.

Page 131, Exercise C

Answers will vary.

Page 132, Exercise A

1. speeding
2. tailgating
3. not wearing a seat belt
4. running a red light
5. talking on a cell phone while driving
6. changing lanes without signaling

Page 132, Exercise B

Officer: Good afternoon. I need to see your _driver's license_ and _registration_.
Driver: OK. Here they are.
Officer: Please _turn off your engine_ and _stay in your car_. I'll be back in a moment.

[a few minutes later]
Officer: I pulled you over for _not wearing a seat belt_. I'm giving you a _warning_ this time. Please drive safely.

Page 133, Exercise C

1. Drive slower and stay at the same speed.
2. Maintain your engine and check the air in your tires.
3. Turn off the engine and empty your trunk.
4. Don't start or stop quickly or get stuck in traffic.
5. Don't run just one errand or use the air-conditioning.

Page 133, Exercise D

Answers will vary.

UNIT 12
Page 134, Exercise A

1. b   4. f
2. c   5. d
3. a   6. e

Page 134, Exercise B

1. wear latex gloves
2. maintain the equipment
3. ask questions
4. clock in / out
5. wash hands
6. call in late

Page 135, Exercise C

1. a   2. c   3. b

Page 135, Exercise D

Answers will vary, but could include:

a waitress:
ask questions
wash hands
clock in and out

a gardener:
maintain the equipment
report problems with the equipment
follow directions

a nurse:
wear latex gloves
work as a team
follow directions

Page 136, Exercise A

Answers will vary, but could include:

1. must wear / must not wear
2. have to smoke / can't smoke
3. must park / must not park
4. have to wear / can't enter
5. can't make / must make
6. must wash
7. have to wear

Page 137, Exercise B

1. must park
2. must not clock
3. have to wear
4. must take
5. must pass
6. have to go
7. have to get
8. can't be late

Page 137, Exercise C

Answers will vary, but could include:

1. Greg has to clock in and out.
2. Greg must wear a uniform.
3. Greg has to eat his lunch in the employee break room.
4. Greg can't smoke cigarettes inside the building.

Page 138, Exercise A

1. B   5. F
2. A   6. C
3. E   7. G
4. D

Page 138, Exercise B

1. $570.00
2. $12.00
3. overtime
4. $440.00
5. 45
6. $130.00
7. 5/15
8. $50.00

Page 139, Exercise C

1. $8.50
2. $12.75
3. 6
4. Social Security
5. $361.50
6. No, it's for two.

Page 139, Exercise D

Description	Hours	Rate of Pay	Earnings
Regular	(30)	$14.00	$490.00

Description	Hours	Rate of Pay	Earnings
Regular	40	$7.50	$300.00
Overtime	5	($7.50)	$ 37.50

Page 140, Exercise A

1. Who worked
2. What time does my shift begin
3. Who did you call
4. Which shift do you prefer
5. Where do you work
6. What time does the store close

Page 140, Exercise B

1. Who do I talk to about my schedule?
   Walter, the assistant manager.
2. When do I take my break?
   Take your break at 12:30.
3. Which days do I have off this week?
   Wednesday and Friday.
4. Where is the break room?
   Second door on the left.

Page 141, Exercise C

1. Which days do you have off?
2. What time do you take your break?
3. Who did you trade shifts with?
4. Where do I store safety gear?
5. When do you need time off?

Page 141, Exercise D

1. At 7 A.M.
2. From 2–3 P.M.
3. Mondays and Fridays
4. At 4 P.M.
5. Viktor and Ana
6. Franco
7. Grocery department
8. Viktor

Page 142, Before You Read

Answers will vary.

Page 143, Exercise A

a

Page 143, Exercise B

1. ask questions / work assignments
2. coworkers / help
3. finish / find
4. supervisor / next time
5. afraid / try

Page 143, Exercise C

1. 3
2. 2
3. 1
4. 4
5. 5

Page 144, Exercise A

1. Can I talk to you for a moment?
2. Could you cover my shift next Saturday?
3. Could you help me store the equipment?
4. Can I ask you about taking some vacation time?
5. Could I change to evenings?

Page 144, Exercise B

1. **Bae:** Hi, Sue. *Could I talk* to you for a minute?
   Sue: Of course. What's up?
   Bae: *Could I leave* work a little early on Thursday? My son is graduating from kindergarten at 4:00.
   Sue: Well, *can you stay* a little later this afternoon?
   Bae: Yes, I *can*. No problem.
2. **Miguel:** *Can you work overtime* on Saturday, Angelica?
   Angel: Well, I take my children to swim class on Saturday mornings.
   Miguel: *Could you come* Saturday afternoon? Janet is out sick and I need someone to cover her hours.
   Angel: Sure. *Can I come* at 1:00?
   Miguel: That's great. Thanks.

Page 145, Exercise C

1. Can / Could I borrow your dictionary?
2. Can / Could I have the morning off?
3. Can / Could I have some overtime hours next week?
4. Can / Could I ask you something?
5. Can / Could you cover my hours this weekend?
6. Can / Could I take a break early?

Page 145, Exercise D

Answers will vary, but could include:

1. Can / Could I have next Wednesday night off?
2. Can / Could I change to the morning shift?
3. Can / Could I leave 15 minutes early?
4. Can / Could I change to the evening shift?

Audio CD Track List